The Forgotten Command:

BE HOLY

To .

Gina

6. 11. 11

Proverbs 3 v 6 .

From . Liz .

The Forgotten Command:
BE HOLY

WILLIAM MACDONALD

JOHN RITCHIE
CHRISTIAN PUBLICATIONS

JOHN RITCHIE LTD.
40 BEANSBURN, KILMARNOCK, SCOTLAND

ISBN 0 946351 37 6

Copyright © 1993 by John Ritchie Ltd.
40 Beansburn, Kilmarnock, Scotland

Second Edition Revised
1995

Third Edition
2002

Typeset by Newtext Composition Ltd, Glasgow.
Printed in Great Britain by Bell and Bain Ltd, Glasgow.

Table of Contents

Introduction

THE FALLOUT among those who profess faith in Christ is appalling. Many seem to be born running; they start out well. But along the line they fall into sin and go into eclipse. Of course, not all who claim to be Christians are genuinely saved, but even among those who demonstrate reality, the casualty rate is sobering.

Too often it happens that a single fall puts a person on the shelf for the rest of his life. In spite of the fact that he repents and confesses his sin, he feels he is under a cloud from then on. He sees himself as unfit for service. He seals his lips as far as testimony is concerned. He goes through life as a self-styled reject. Our churches are filled with people like this.

It doesn't have to be so. There is forgiveness with God. The bird with the broken wing *can* fly as high again. God *can* restore the years that the locusts have eaten. The trouble seems to be that many have never learned how to appropriate forgiveness. They confess their sins but they do not believe God's word that they have been forgiven. Perhaps they don't *feel* forgiven. Or perhaps they know that they have been forgiven but they can't forgive *themselves*. And so they go through life as defeated Christians.

This book is written to help people like that. But it is also written to steer believers away from ever getting into that position in the first place. Experience is a costly school. If we are willing to learn directly from the word of God, we need not learn the hard way. Through simple obedience to the Bible, a Christian may know all the blessings of a holy life and avoid all the hurtful consequences of sin. Why should we learn through shame and disgrace what is so obvious to anyone who takes the time to study the Bible?

CHAPTER 1

Christlikeness

THE HIGHEST description of character is the word *Christlike*. When applied to a believer, it is the ideal tribute, the ultimate honour. There is no ambition higher than the desire to be like the Lord Jesus.

Henry Drummond said, "To become like Christ is the only thing in the world worth caring for, the thing before which every ambition of man is folly, and all lower achievement vain."

> To be like Jesus, to be like Jesus!
>   All I ask to be like Him!
> All through life's journey from earth to glory,
>   All I ask to be like Him.
>
> *Anonymous*

I am sure it must be satisfying to be extremely gifted, to teach or preach in such a way that all hearts are bowed and stirred beneath the influence of the Word. But Christlikeness is better than great gift, and without it, the gift is a resounding gong or a clanging cymbal. It is possible to be gifted in the pulpit and a perfect grouch at home. Gift is a sovereign favour of God in a person's life, but personal grace is something that we have a responsibility to develop by the power of the Holy Spirit.

Many aspire to be great personal soul winners. Indeed this ministry is so popularised today that it is practically touted as the purpose of our creation. The result is that we have people rushing around in

1

breathless personal evangelism, yet their lives make the christian faith look very unattractive and unconvincing. When Jesus said, "Follow Me, and I will make you fishers of men," He gave the proper order and the proper priority. Our responsibility is to follow Him, that is, to live as He lived. His responsibility is to make us fishers of men. Soul-winning is the natural outcome of Christlikeness.

The Divine Priority

God's great purpose as far as His people are concerned is to conform them to the image of His Son. He is so pleased with Jesus that He wants to fill heaven with others who are like Him. When we see Him, we will be automatically changed into His likeness. But there is more glory for God if the process is going on now.

Two unforgettable illustrations of this process have been given by Carole Mayhall. The first is of a rather obese woman who enrolled in a reducing programme.

The first thing the supervisor did was draw a silhouette on a mirror in the shape she wished to become. As she stood before the mirror, she bulged out over the silhouette. The instructor told her, "Our goal is for you to fit this shape." For many weeks the woman dieted and exercised. Each week she would stand in front of the mirror, but her volume, while decreasing, still overflowed. And so she exercised harder and dieted more rigidly. Finally one day, to everyone's delight, as she stood in front of the mirror she was conformed to the image of the silhouette.

The second illustration is of a sculptor who fashioned a lion out of a block of granite. When asked how he had accomplished such a wonderful masterpiece he replied, "It was easy. All I did was to chip away everything that didn't look like a lion!"

In the following pages, we will describe how God's goal is to chisel away on our lives until the image of the Man appears. As we read on, may our prayer be:

> Let it be seen that with Thee I have been,
>   Jesus, my Lord and my Saviour;
> Let it be known I am only Thine own
>   By all my speech and behaviour.

CHAPTER 2

Poor Role Models of Christ

EVERY CHRISTIAN is intended to represent the Lord Jesus here on earth. He is to be a role model of the Saviour, showing the world what Christ is like. It is an awesome responsibility.

We are members of the body of Christ. The body is the vehicle by which a person expresses himself. Christ's body, the Church, is the vehicle by which He chooses to reveal Himself to the world.

That raises the question for each one of us, "What kind of picture of Christ do I give?" It causes us to ask ourselves:

> If of Jesus Christ their only view
> May be what they see of Him in you,
> My soul, what do they see?

Someone put it this way. God has a surname. He is called the God of Abraham, Isaac and Jacob. He is not ashamed to be called their God (Heb 11:16b). How would He feel about having my name as His last name?

Said Charles Swindoll:

> Like it or not, the world watches us with the scrutiny of a seagull peering at a shrimp in shallow water. The believer ... is under constant surveillance. That's our number one occupational hazard. And when we speak of our Saviour and

the life He offers, everything we say is filtered through that which has been observed by others.

Wounded in the House of His Friends

The sad fact is that Christ has suffered greatly by the lives of those who profess to be His disciples. He has been wounded in the house of His friends.

Said James Spink:

> More evil is done to the cause of Christianity by its adherents than its opponents, for the world often contrasts a Christian's profession with his practice. They argue rightly that if Christianity is what we claim it is, it ought to make a difference in the life.

Hudson Taylor concurred:

> The inconsistencies of christian people, who while professing to believe their Bibles, were yet content to live just as they would if there were no such Book, had been one of the strongest arguments of my sceptical companions.

It is not hard to find illustrations of how the Lord Jesus is misrepresented. I saw a pickup truck recently with two stickers on the back bumper. One said, "I love Jesus." The one on the right, affecting an Italian style, said "You toucha my car, I breaka your face." Apparently the owner did not sense the glaring contradiction between the two sentiments.

Move on to the business world. George Duncan tells the following story:

> ... a businessman ... had been involved in a christian broadcast the night before, and a girl he

employed had heard it. That morning he was in a very bad mood, things were not going well, and for some reason the girl got the benefit of his temper. As she went out of the office, she said to another girl who was coming in, "That's right ... Come to Jesus on Sunday night and go to hell on Monday morning."

When a christian businessman reneged on a commitment, his competitor asked him, "What kind of a church do you belong to?" He answered, "Leave my church out of this. This has nothing to do with church. This is business." It may have taken twenty years to establish his testimony, but it was destroyed in twenty seconds.

When a famous actor or actress agrees to be "born again," the news is broadcast coast to coast. But so is the news when he does not make a clean break with his former lifestyle, when he stars in a low-grade movie, when it is evident that Christ has not made a difference in his life.

Or it could be "christian musicians" with their theatrical performances, suggestive body language, questionable lyrics, and music that apes the world's. This is Christianity? Or is it a parody, a ridiculous imitation?

A gangster professed to be converted at a large evangelistic rally. The news spread like wildfire. But he continued to carry on his underworld activities. When someone confronted him with this caricature of Christianity, he said, "No one told me that in saying yes to Jesus, I would be turning my back on my former life. After all, there are christian football players, christian cowboys, christian politicians. Why not a christian gangster?" Since then he has abandoned Christianity.

Then there are the christian TV personalities sporting costly coiffures, dripping with jewellery, and made up like Jezebel. This is the way Jesus is presented, not as my penniless friend from Nazareth.

Pass the Loot

And don't forget those radio and TV preachers who carry on a begging, money-making racket, live in sumptuous homes and travel in expensive cars and planes. Soon a clever reporter exposes the whole game for what it is, and Christianity suffers another smear.

One of America's favourite TV preachers was reported to live in a twelve-room mansion modelled after the Palace of Versailles with fabulous formal gardens, stables and pools. Another bought a half-million-dollar mansion in Los Angeles, which his wife called a little place to get away to. He added a Rolls Royce to his fleet of Mercedes and Jaguars.

It is heartbreaking to hear how many christian leaders, at the pinnacle of the religious ladder, have hit the headlines with sex scandals. Some have run off with their secretaries and divorced their wives. Or how many celebrated christian women have turned away from home and husband to live with another man? The evangelical world really needs a thorough house-cleaning.

I think how Christ is sometimes libelled by "christian politicians", with their earthy language, their questionable compromises, their shadowy associations. The dishonour done to the name of Jesus is incalculable.

Perhaps we should also mention famous prisoners who claim to have been saved. Through strong representations from believers, a doubting, reluctant judge agrees to release them. Some christian organization latches on to them and puts them on the preaching circuit (to raise money for the organization). Before long they fall again and are back inside.

Christian students who cheat on exams, housewives who quarrel with their neighbours, common folks who are rude and short-tempered all are libels instead of Bibles. Every instance of behaviour that is un-Christlike causes His enemies to blaspheme. Every poor role model causes the unconverted to say, "What you are speaks so loud, I can't hear what you say." It was this kind of conduct that caused John MacArthur to say, "I think that Jesus had more class than a lot of His agents have."

A soldier was brought before Alexander the Great for disobeying orders.

> "What is your name?" demanded Alexander.
> "Alexander", the soldier replied sheepishly.
> "Alexander? Then either change your name or change your ways!" ordered the great military leader.

Those of us who bear the name of *Christian* should act accordingly. "It is inconsistent to say you believe as you should when you behave as you shouldn't"

(H. G. Bosch).

In conversation with Mahatma Gandhi one day, E. Stanley Jones said:

> "I am very anxious to see Christianity naturalized in India, so that it shall be no longer a foreign thing identified with a foreign people and a foreign government, but a part of the national life of India and contributing its power to India's uplift and redemption. What would you suggest that we do to make that possible?" Gandhi gravely and thoughtfully replied, "I would suggest ... that all of you Christians ... must begin to live more like Jesus Christ. Secondly, I would suggest that you must practice your religion without adulterating or toning it down. Third, I would suggest that you must put your emphasis upon love, for love is the centre and soul of Christianity."

It is reported that Ghandi once said, "If it weren't for the Christians, I would have become one."

Brian Goodwin tells of

> a young Chinese who was educated by a missionary at a christian school. He admired his teacher and when, some years later, he heard that the teacher had come back to town, he tried to contact him in the hotel where he was staying. He was refused access to the missionary, however, and thrown out of the hotel. "So that's how Christians act, he muttered as he walked away. All the years of care and attention heaped upon him by his missionary teacher were neutralized by this great humiliation. The name of the young Chinese was Mao Tse-tung.

So much for the bad news. But thank God this is not the whole story.

CHAPTER 3

People Who Make Us Think Of Jesus

IN THE last chapter we discussed how true Christians and nominal Christians often grossly misrepresent the Saviour to the world. It was rather depressing. But, praise God, there is another side to the picture. There are men and women who have given a faithful picture of God's Son to those around them.

I think of one of my students who was also a close friend. Though he was dying of melanoma, his bedroom was a little anteroom of heaven. When a district nurse made one of her periodic visits, she said, "Rob reminds me of Jesus."

Robert C. Chapman humbly set before himself this great aim: "Seeing so many preach Christ, and so few live Christ, I will aim to live Christ." Later John Nelson Darby said of him, "He lives what I teach."

Speaking of William Arnot, a friend said, "His preaching was good, his writing better, but his life, best of all."

When Sadhu Singh, a converted Sikh, rang the doorbell at a Christian's house, the maid opened the door, then ran to her mistress with the excited announcement that Christ had come. In another home, he made a tremendous impression on the children when he played on the floor with them. That night they asked their mother if Jesus could put them to bed. Said his biographer, "They were only expressing in words the thoughts of all who met him. His Christlike appearance was matched by his gentleness and the authority of his bearing and spirit."

A Jesus-Like Man

In a biography of Robert Murray McCheyne, James A. Stewart wrote:

> Mr. McCheyne's holiness was noticeable even before he spoke a word; his appearance spoke for him. There was a minister in the North of Scotland with whom he spent the night. He was so marvellously struck by this about him that when Mr. McCheyne left the room, he burst into tears and said, "Oh, that is the most Jesus-like man I ever saw."

In another place, Stewart adds:

> McCheyne spent hours in holy communion inside the Veil, in rapturous praise and adoration, being bathed in Calvary's Love. He would come forth from God's presence to leave the fragrance of Christ as he went from house to house in visitation. As he walked the streets of his parish – and even anywhere in Britain – the people were startled to see the look of Jesus upon his face.

Sally Magnusson writes that Eric Liddell, the great Scottish runner and missionary, was like his Lord when he was interned in a Japanese concentration camp.

> What they keep coming back to again and again, these people, is the way he lived his Christianity. Eric is portrayed as the Christ-figure here at the

camp just as much as he was among the Chinese in Siaochang. He befriends the prostitute, and the despised businessman; he carries coal for the weak and teaches the young; he gets ready to sell his gold watch and tears up his sheets for hockey sticks. And yet he is the same Eric ... looking extremely ordinary and nothing special at all.

Richard Hillary, in his book *The Last Enemy,* frankly confessed that he was both annoyed and challenged by Peter Pease, a fellow-pilot – a professed Christian and the best man he had ever met. His one ambition was to get him alone, to attack him mercilessly and tear the fabric of his faith to pieces. His chance came as they travelled together in a railway compartment from Montrose to Edinburgh. He glared at his victim and said, "Your religion is a fake, a hereditary hangover, a useful social adjunct and no more." Peter opened his mouth, stammered out a few feeble protests, then lapsed into silence crushed by his opponent's flood of dialectics. But Hillary knew that in reality he had lost the argument, for there was one fact he could not explain - Peter's character. It and his religion were inextricably bound up together, and it played havoc with logic.

That is why J. H. Jowett wrote:

Men may more than match you in subtlety of argument. In intellectual argument you may suffer an easy defeat. But the argument of a redeemed life is unassailable. "Seeing the man that was healed standing with them, they could say nothing against it."

R.W. DeHaan wrote:

> Shortly after arriving on the field, a missionary was speaking for the first time to a group of villagers. He was trying to present the gospel to them. In describing Jesus Christ, he referred to Him as a man who was compassionate, kind, loving, caring, and one who went about doing good. While he was speaking, he noticed that his lesson brought smiles of familiarity to the faces of his audience as they nodded their heads in agreement. Somewhat puzzled, he interrupted his message to ask: "Do you know who I'm talking about?" One of the villagers quickly responded, "Yes, we do. You've been talking about a man who used to come here." Eagerly they told about a missionary doctor who had come to their remote village to minister to their physical needs. His life had been so Christlike in caring for the people that they saw the Lord Jesus in him. He was truly an example of conforming to Christ.

Sir Henry M. Stanley said:

> I went to Africa as prejudiced against religion as the worst infidel in London. To a reporter like myself, who had only to deal with wars, mass meetings, and political gatherings, sentimental matters were quite out of my province. But there came to me a long time for reflection. I was out there away from a worldly world. I saw the solitary old man, David Livingstone, and I asked myself, "Why does he stay here in such a place? What is it that inspires him?"
>
> For months after we met, I found myself listening to him, wondering at the old man carrying out the words, "Leave all and follow Me." But little by little, seeing his piety, his gentleness, his zeal, his earnestness, and how he went quietly about his

business, I was converted by him although he had not tried in any way to do it.

R.C. Sproul tells of a time when Billy Graham played golf with President Gerald Ford, Jack Nicklaus, and another pro. Later the pro complained to a friend that he didn't need to have Billy cramming religion down his throat. He thereupon made for the driving range and took out his anger on a bucket of golf balls. When his friend followed and asked, "Was Billy a little rough on you out there?" the pro sighed and said with embarrassment, "No, he didn't even mention religion." Sproul explains, "Astonishingly, Billy Graham had said nothing about God, Jesus, or religion, yet the pro stomped away after the game, accusing Billy of trying to ram religion down his throat. What had happened? Simply this: The evangelist had so reflected Christlikeness that his presence made the pro feel uncomfortable."

One day when some missionaries to India were entertaining their fellow missionary Silas Fox, a Hindu neighbour came in, met Mr. Fox, had a brief visit with him, then departed. After he left, she rushed back and said excitedly, "I saw the God in his face." She who believed in many gods saw the one and only true God in the face of Silas Fox.

But we know that holiness does not come upon people effortlessly. It involves the human will. Believers must want to be holy, and must discipline themselves toward that end. They must be motivated. And that raises the question, "What is it that moves men to pursue holiness?"

Read on!

CHAPTER 4

Why Be Holy?

WHY DOES a believer desire to be more holy? Why is his theme song, "More like the Master I would ever be?" Why does he agonise with a passion for Christlikeness?

Well, first of all, it is an instinct that is built into him at the time of his conversion. He receives a new hatred of sin and a new love of purity. The indwelling Holy Spirit yearns within to reproduce a sanctified character. The new nature manifests itself in a craving for victory in the personal life.

But in addition to that, there are very strong reasons why a Christian should pursue holiness, why he should resist the temptations of the world, the flesh, and the devil.

One of the worst things about sin is the dishonour it brings on the name of the Lord Jesus. The outside world is justified in associating the disciple with his Master. If the disciple sins, people reproach the Master and drag His name in the mud. Shameful behaviour is linked in their minds with Him. In 1987, when a TV preacher became involved in a sex scandal, the country's best-known atheist said it was "just another example of why religion is a bad, ugly, nasty game." By his sins of adultery and murder, David brought endless blasphemy on the name of the Lord (2 Sam 12:14). Victor Jack listed four things that died when David sinned: The smile on the face of God died – "the thing ... displeased the Lord" (2

Sam 11:27); the peace in David's heart died – "I have sinned"; the stability of David's throne died – "the sword shall never depart from your house"; his witness before the world died – "you have given great occasion to the enemies of the Lord to blaspheme."

Another motive for holiness is the memory of what our sins cost the Saviour (1 Pet 2:24). No thinking believer would want to go on in that which nailed the Son of God to the cross. If the shedding of His blood was necessary to pay sin's penalty, how can His followers ever tolerate or condone iniquity?

Christ's love for us should constrain us to live in purity. He loved us when we were ungodly enemies. He demonstrated His love by paying an enormous price to redeem us. He has provided everything necessary for a life of godliness. He couldn't love us more than He does. It is a miserable response to such love to go back over the bridge to our former way of life.

We forget all too easily what has been called the forgotten commandment, "Be ye holy, for I am holy" (Lev 11:44; 1 Pet 1:16). Peter leaves us in no doubt: that commandment may have been found in the OT, but it matters today. God's standard of holiness is Himself, and anyone who has looked carefully at His Son must admit that He is the standard.

Sin Breaks God's Heart

Our love for Christ should make us desire to be clean vessels, fit for His use. If we really love Him, we will want to please Him. Sin not only breaks His law, but His heart as well, whereas holiness delights Him. He said, "If you love Me, keep My commandments" (Jn 14:15). Holiness is commanded (1 Pet 1:15, 16; Heb 12:14).

Sin makes other people stumble, both unbelievers and believers. When the unsaved see a Christian fall, they conclude that the gospel doesn't make a difference in a person's life after all and they turn away. Not only do they decide against following the Lord but they actively ridicule the Christian faith. Mark Twain turned away from Christianity because he heard Christians condoning slavery, using foul language, and engaging in shady deals. Mahummad received the conception of one true God from Jews and Christians, but he was turned off by their lives. Comments Brian Goodwin, "A little more love to Christ and to others might have changed the course of history for what is now the Muslim world."

When we sin, it stumbles other believers; they are disappointed and let down. It hurts people who have trusted us, whether in the family or the church. Our family must bear some of the shame and hurt. Our local church receives unwelcome publicity when our sin is public, but even secret sin lowers its spiritual tone and effectiveness. A young believer feels betrayed and shattered when the one who led him to the Lord brings disgrace on himself. How often have Christians been saved from stumbling by the vision of supportive, believing friends flashing across their minds!

The life of holiness is the best life – best for the spirit, soul, and body. It is good for physical and emotional health. It saves us from remorse, guilt, shame and many forms of disease. It leads to fullness of joy and pleasures for evermore (1 John 1:4; Ps 16:11). When a little boy emerged from a meeting with a sad look, someone asked him what was the matter. He replied, "It's hard to be happy and holy at the same time." But the truth is that without holiness, there can be no true happiness.

The constant realisation that our body is the temple of the Holy Spirit should motivate us to "cleanse ourselves from all filthiness of the flesh and spirit, perfecting holiness in the fear of God" (2 Cor 7:1). We should never lose a sense of amazement that one of the members of the Godhead is our permanent Indweller and constant Companion.

Godliness has "promise of the life that now is, but also of that which is to come" (1 Tim 4:8). It is the best preparation for eternity. Some day, perhaps soon, we are going to see the Lord Jesus. We are going to stand before His Judgment Seat. That means that we should be living now in the light of that awe-inspiring event. That, in turn, can only point to a life of holiness.

Sin Seals the Lips

Holiness gives liberty in serving the Lord whereas sin seals the lips. The guilt and sense of unfitness that accompany unconfessed sin paralyse a person. He does not enjoy the release of the Spirit. His witness is temporarily destroyed, and his credibility is called into question.

Holiness gives confidence in prayer. "If our heart does not condemn us, then we have confidence toward God. And whatever we ask we receive from

Him, because we keep His commandments and do those things that are pleasing in His sight" (1 John 3:21, 22). The flip side of this is that if we regard iniquity in our heart, the Lord will not hear us (Ps 66:18). Sin disconnects the prayer line.

And it breaks fellowship with God. This may not sound serious but it is. The believer who is following at a distance is in constant peril. He may make a decision, enter a relationship, or yield to a temptation that will put him on the shelf and cast a cloud over the rest of his life.

The fear of God is a motivation for holiness; it should be a powerful one. The expression "the fear of God" has been so toned down that it means nothing more than respect or reverence. Perhaps the time has come to say that it also means fear – a healthy fear of God, a fear of displeasing Him, a fear of His discipline. There is still a sense in which the Lord visits the iniquity of a father to the third and fourth generation; many a father who has been unfaithful to his wife has lived to see his sin repeated by his son.

These then are some of the reasons why we should never relax in the pursuit of holiness and why we should be highly motivated to grow in likeness to our blessed Redeemer.

Now it is time for us to examine the subject of sanctification in greater detail. And remember – sanctification is just another word for holiness.

CHAPTER 5

Four Kinds of Sanctification

JOE DIDN'T know it but he was marked out by the Holy Spirit before he was saved. Actually he was set apart from before the time he was born. As he grew up, things happened that didn't seem significant at the time. He came in contact with true believers. One day a stranger handed him a gospel tract. He accidentally tuned into a christian broadcast. A fellow witnessed to him at work. He watched a gospel crusade on TV. Then his wife was converted, and his home was radically changed. Later he would realise that the Holy Spirit was arranging these "coincidences" as links in the chain of his salvation.

When Joe finally trusted Jesus Christ as Lord and Saviour, he learned that he was given a position of sanctification before God. God now saw him "in Christ." That means that Christ was now his holiness, and because of that, he was fit for heaven. He was no longer a member of the world system headed by Satan. Now he was a member of Christ, set apart from the world.

Joe began to notice changes in his life. He had a new hatred of sin and a new longing for holiness. He still sinned, but not as before. Sin didn't rule his life. He no longer sinned with the full consent of his will. And when he did, he was ashamed to his tiptoes. His old habits began to drop off. His speech underwent a

thorough cleaning. No doubt about it! He was growing in holiness.

Joe died last Tuesday. When he saw the Saviour
face to face, the miraculous transformation took place.
Joe became like Jesus morally and spiritually. He
was forever freed from all sin and defilement.

Let's Get the Meaning Straight

These four chapters in Joe's life illustrate the four
aspects of sanctification that are found in the NT.
But before we get to that, let us think about what the
word "sanctification" means in general.

Sanctification is another word for holiness. Both
are translations of the same word in the original
language of the NT and they have the same meaning.

To be holy or sanctified is to be set apart. That is
the only definition that will suit every occurrence in
the Bible.

It is a common mistake to think that to sanctify
means to make more perfect. This cannot be true
because we read that Jesus sanctified Himself (John
17:19) and we are to sanctify Him in our hearts (1
Pet 3:15). He could not make Himself more perfect
than He is, and we certainly cannot add to His
perfection. But He could and did set Himself apart to
the work to which His Father called Him, and we can
set Him apart in our lives as Sovereign Lord and
God.

In the Bible, sanctification or holiness is used of
persons and things. All three members of the God-

head are holy, that is, set apart from all created beings in the excellence of their character and conduct (Lev 11:44-45; John 10:36; 1 Cor 6:19). Mount Sinai was sanctified in the sense that it was set apart as the place where the law was given (Exod 19:23). In the Old Testament God sanctified the seventh day (Gen 2:3); it was set apart as a day of rest from labour. The firstborn of both men and animals were sanctified to the Lord (Exod 13:2) and set apart as belonging to Him. The tabernacle and all its furniture were sanctified, that is, set apart for divine service (Exod 40:9). The people of Israel sanctified themselves to do iniquity (Isa 66:17). They obviously didn't make themselves more holy, in the common sense of the word.

There is a sense in which even unbelievers can be sanctified. For example, "the unbelieving husband is sanctified by the wife" (1 Cor 7:14). This does not mean that his salvation is assured. All it means is that he is set apart in a position of external privilege because he has a christian wife. The influence of a believing, praying partner is a great benefit.

From this it is clear that the words "set apart" cover all uses of sanctification.

Now to get back to the four aspects of sanctification that are found in the NT. These are known as:

> Pre-conversion sanctification.
> Positional sanctification.
> Practical or progressive sanctification.
> Perfect sanctification.

Pre-conversion Sanctification

All believers were sanctified by the Holy Spirit before they were saved. Paul describes three steps in the salvation of the Thessalonians (2 Thess 2:13).

> Their selection by God.
> Their sanctification by the Spirit.
> Their belief of the truth.

Peter gives a similar list in 1 Peter 1:2:

> Choice and destiny by God the Father.
> Sanctification by the Spirit.
> Obedience to Jesus Christ.
> Sprinkling with His blood.

In both cases, sanctification comes before conversion. The Holy Spirit sets the person apart to belong to Christ. Then the person obeys the truth, and the value of the sprinkled blood of Christ is credited to his account.

Positional Sanctification

The moment a person is saved, he is sanctified positionally, that is, God sees him in Christ, set apart from the world for Himself (1 Cor 1:2). In a very real sense, Christ is his sanctification (1 Cor 1:30).

Every true believer is a saint; he has been set apart for God. One child defined a saint as a dead Christian. On the contrary, every true Christian, living or dead, is a saint. But he may be carnal at the same time (1 Cor 1:1, 2; 3:1, 3). He may be sanctified positionally but not very saintly in his behaviour. Sanctified people are later exhorted to be holy (1 Pet 1:2, 15, 16).

In Acts 20:32, the expression "all those who are sanctified" means all believers. In Acts 26:18 the Lord described His people as "those who are sanctified by faith in Me." The Corinthians are described as having been "washed ... sanctified ... justified" (1 Cor 6:11). These passages all refer to positional sanctification.

Practical or Progressive Sanctification

But then there is practical sanctification. This refers to what we should be in our everyday lives. We should be living lives of separation to God from sin and evil. Whenever we are exhorted to be holy, the reference is to practical sanctification. This is the aspect of holiness that we usually talk about.

Jesus referred to it in John 17:17 when He prayed for His own: "Sanctify them by Your truth. Your word is truth." Paul urged the Corinthians "... let us cleanse ourselves from all filthiness of the flesh and spirit, perfecting holiness in the fear of God" (2 Cor 7:1). In the same vein Peter wrote, "... as He who called you is holy, you also be holy in all your conduct" (1 Pet 1:15).

If we are going to be set apart, we will inevitably be different from the unsaved people around us. Sometimes this is a hard truth to swallow. We don't want to be different. We want to be like the herd. We want to merge into our own surroundings. But God wants us to be different.

When God called Israel, He wanted them to be, as Balaam said, "a people dwelling alone, not reckoning itself among the nations" (Num 23:9b). In many ways He taught them the truth of separation. They were not to sow their fields with mixed seeds (Lev 19:19). They were not to wear garments made with a mixture of wool and linen (Lev 19:19). They were not to plough with an ox and a donkey yoked together (Deut 22:10).

But Israel didn't want to be different. Soon the people were clamouring for a king *like the other nations* (1 Sam 8:5, 20).

The parallel with the Church today does not need elaboration.

Perfect Sanctification

The fourth aspect is perfect sanctification. This is still future for the believer. When he sees the Saviour face to face, he will be forever set apart from all sin and defilement (1 John 3:2). He will be morally like the Lord Jesus – perfectly sanctified.

That is what we read about in Col 1:22: "in the body of His flesh through death, to present you holy, and blameless, and irreproachable in His sight."

In another passage, Jude reminds us that our Lord will present us "faultless before the presence of His glory with exceeding joy" (Jude 24).

These then are the four aspects of sanctification: what happened before conversion; what happened at the time of conversion; what is happening day by day; and what will happen when we see the Lord. It is the third aspect that concerns us primarily in this book. The next chapter, for instance, deals with the development of christian character using the figure of military equipment.

CHAPTER 6

The Whole Armour of God

THERE ARE various illustrations of holiness in the New Testament.

Holiness is like taking off old, soiled clothes and putting on new, fresh clothes (Col 3:9, 10). The new clothes are actually the life of Christ. We are to "put on the Lord Jesus Christ, and make no provision for the flesh, to fulfil its lusts" (Rom 13:14).

Another picture of holiness is the fruit that grows on the vine. Christ is the Vine. As the believer abides in Him, he produces the fruit of a Christlike character (John 15:1-17). Paul speaks of this as the fruit of the Spirit (Gal 5:22, 23).

At one moment Paul sees holiness as love incarnated in Christ and then in the believer (1 Cor 13). In the next minute his fertile mind uses the picture of a soldier's armour (Eph 6:10-18). Let us see how he develops this picture.

Why We Need Armour

The christian life is a warfare and each believer is a soldier. The battle rages constantly although at times the assault is more furious than at others. Those soldiers who are totally committed to their Captain, who stand closest to Him, are special targets. The enemy does not waste his ammunition on nominal believers.

The final outcome is assured. "We are more than conquerors through him who loved us" (Rom 8:37). If the Lord is for us, no one can be successfully against us (see Rom 8:31). Eventually every hostile power will bow the knee to our Jesus and confess that He is Lord, to the glory of God the Father (see Phil 2:11).

But why then do we see the corpses of so many of our comrades littering the battlefield? Why have so many well-known preachers and teachers been knocked out of the battle? Why has our casualty rate been so high? The answer, of course, is that the enemy found a chink in their armour and he aimed straight for it.

We are all in danger of going down to defeat, just as others have done. To guard us against it, the Apostle Paul has given a short military manual in Eph 6:10-18. It contains all that is necessary to see us safely and successfully through the conflict.

His Strength, Not Ours

First we must be strong in the Lord, and in the power of His might (v.10). We are flirting with death if we charge forth depending on our own strength. The enemy has supernatural power. In ourselves we are helpless to overcome him. Our greatest resource is to acknowledge our own weakness and to allow His power to flow through us. Isn't that what Paul meant when he said, "... when I am weak, then I am strong" (2 Cor 12:10)? God's strength is made perfect in our weakness (2 Cor 12:9). And when weak soldiers emerge on the winning side, the glory all belongs to the One who empowered them.

The Whole Armour

But we must also put on the whole armour of God. As we shall see, this consists of a belt, a breastplate, shoes or sandals, a shield, a helmet, a sword, and plenty of prayer. Perhaps as Paul wrote this he was looking at the uniform of a Roman soldier guarding him, and he drew a spiritual parallel from it. So we must ask ourselves the question, "What is the spiritual counterpart of the Roman armour?" Certainly it is not literal military hardware, because "the weapons of our warfare are not carnal but mighty in God for pulling down strongholds" (2 Cor 10:4). Some think it refers to our position in Christ. For example, they say that the breastplate of righteousness is the righteousness with which God clothes us when we are born again. If the armour referred to the righteousness, truth, faith and salvation which are ours because of our relationship to Christ, then all believers would be invulnerable. We would never hear of Christians falling on the field because of immorality or false doctrine. There would be no necessity for the christian troops to put on anything, because they would always be outfitted with the armour. No, it cannot refer to our position in Christ. It must have to do with our daily life and practice.

We believe that the armour of God describes the elements of strong christian character. If the christian soldier cultivates all the marks of a blameless life, then the enemy has little to shoot at. The fact that we are commanded to put on the armour shows that there are positive things that we must do. It is a question of what kind of soldiers we are and how we behave.

The Devil's Devices

The armour of God enables us to hold our ground against the wiles of the devil (v.11b). Satan is a crafty foe, employing unimaginably clever tricks against God's people. We must know our enemy and be constantly on guard against his devilish stratagems. What are some of his demonic tricks?

He is a liar, the father of lies, and has been so from the beginning (John 8:44). He lied to Eve by misrepresenting God and he has been lying about God ever since.

He is a deceiver. He poses as an angel of light and sends out his messengers posing as ministers of righteousness (2 Cor 11:14, 15). Sometimes he deceives by misquoting the Bible, and at other times by using great miracles and lying wonders (2 Thess 2:9). As a deceiving serpent, he seeks to sow doubts and denials, and to divert God's people from sincere and pure devotion to Christ (2 Cor 11:3).

He is a slanderer, the accuser of the brothers (Rev 12:10). All who slander the Lord's people are doing the devil's work.

He is an imitator. He has a counterfeit for everything that is of God. He empowered the Egyptian magicians to imitate the miracles of Moses (2 Tim 3:8).

He sows discouragement. Paul warned the Corinthians that if they did not forgive the repentant backslider, Satan might gain an advantage by plunging the brother into extreme discouragement (2 Cor 2:7-11). The devil knows that God seldom uses a discouraged person.

One of his favourite strategies is to divide and conquer. He seeks to sow disunity among saints, knowing that a house divided against itself cannot stand.

Satan sometimes appears as a roaring lion to terrify and to devour (1 Pet 5:8). His goal and the goal of all his demons is to destroy. He persecutes the Church (Rev 2:10). He also seeks to destroy men through drugs, spiritism, alcohol, immorality and related vices.

Just as the devil, speaking through Peter, sought to dissuade Jesus from going to the cross (Mark 8:31-33) so he encourages Christians to spare themselves from the shame, suffering, and death connected with cross-bearing.

Often he attacks most viciously right after great spiritual victories and mountain-top experiences, when the danger of pride is greatest.

The Hosts of Satan

Clearly then our battle is not against flesh and blood, though we often have to contend with false teachers, cultists, hostile government agents, and enemies of the truth. The warfare is with the devil and his subordinates, whom Paul identifies as principalities, powers, the world-rulers of this darkness, and the spiritual hosts of wickedness in the heavenly places (v.12). Here is a reminder that our universe is populated with unseen, evil spirit beings, perhaps fallen angels. They obviously have a chain of command, just as any military organisation does. We do not know the order in which they are ranked, but they are all ultimately under Satan's command. These demonic powers use evil men as their puppets to hinder the work of God and to persecute His servants.

When Paul says that we wrestle against these evil powers of darkness, he does not mean that they are our only enemies. Our three basic foes are the world, the flesh, and the devil. But here the apostle is thinking primarily about our warfare with the devil and his hosts.

Stand Your Ground

We need the whole armour of God if we are to stand our ground. The enemy, though not omniscient, has a vast intelligence network and knows where we are most vulnerable. No part of our character can be neglected.

In 2 Sam 23:9, 10, we read of a man named Eleazar who stood his ground and struck the Philistines until his arm was weary and his hand froze to the sword. That is the kind of perseverance and determination that we need in our own lives.

Now Paul is ready to take up the individual pieces of the armour. Some teachers suggest that the first three form the basic uniform while the next three are used in active combat.

The Belt of Truth

The first piece is the belt of truth. The usual explanation of the purpose of the belt is that the soldier tucked his long robe under it so that it would not get in his way. If that is the thought here, then the

Christian uses the word of truth to get rid of anything that would hinder him in the good fight of faith. Jesus warned His disciples against dissipation, drunkenness, and the cares of this life (Luke 21:34). Paul warned that no soldier on active duty entangles himself in the affairs of this life (2 Tim 2:4). We need the belt of truth to protect us from covetousness, wealth, materialism, fame, the lust for power, pleasure-loving and luxurious living.

The belt also suggests that we must hold the truth. We must hold tenaciously to the verbal, plenary inspiration of the Scriptures. We must hold that the Word is without error, as originally given. We must never let a shade of doubt cross our minds concerning this fact – the Bible is the living word of God. We must never let our minds sit in judgment on the Scriptures, but rather let the Scriptures judge our minds.

But it is not enough for us to hold the truth. The truth must hold us. It must control our lives. Practically, this means that we must spend time in the Bible each day. It means that we must obey the Word. It is not enough to obey the passages that suit us. We must obey every command addressed to us. Perhaps most cases of failure in the Christian warfare have resulted from neglect of the Bible. It is true that "this Book will keep you from sin, or sin will keep you from this Book."

There is tremendous security for the believer when he clings to the truth of God's word, when he obeys the truth, and when he manifests the truth by a life of consistent honesty and integrity.

The Breastplate of Righteousness

The second piece of armour is the breastplate of righteousness. In simple language, this means doing what is right in the sight of God and of man. It means having a sensitive conscience to avoid anything that is wrong, shady, or questionable. When we have the breastplate of righteousness on, we refuse to make little compromises that open the way for larger abuses.

We avoid bribes, payoffs, or kickbacks. We are scrupulously honest in filing income tax returns. We would rather fail an exam than cheat in it. We obey the law. We resist the temptation to pad the expense account.

The Lord Jesus wore the breastplate of righteousness at all times (Isa 59:17), and He is our example.

The Gospel Sandals

Then there is the footgear, called "the preparation of the gospel of peace" (v.15). What does this mean? It means a readiness and eagerness to share the gospel. We put on this footwear by praying each morning, "Lord Jesus, lead me to some soul today. Open the door so that I can speak to someone about You." Then if someone indicates that he has a deep, spiritual need, we are ready to lead him to Christ step by step. We have memorised verses about man's sin, Christ's work, and the sinner's responsibility, and the Holy Spirit can direct us in choosing just the right ones.

An old saint was taken to the hospital, seriously ill. When his family visited him the next day and asked, "How are you?" he replied, "Fine! I've spoken to everyone at this end of the ward about the Lord." His feet were shod with the preparation of the gospel of peace.

The Shield of Faith

The fourth piece of equipment is the shield of faith. Its purpose is to quench all the fiery darts of the evil one (v.16). The devil comes to us with doubts about the Scriptures, doubts about the goodness of God, doubts about our own salvation, discouragements, temptations to sin, false accusations, and evil fantasies. We use the shield of faith when we stand firmly on the word of God, obeying its precepts and claiming its promises. Then Satan's darts fall harmlessly to the ground.

God had promised Paul that he would stand before Caesar, but now the ship on which he was travelling to Rome seemed in danger of sinking. Grasping the shield of faith, Paul said, "I believe God, that it shall be even as it was told me" (Acts 27:25).

The Helmet of Salvation

"And take the helmet of salvation" (v.17a). Since a helmet protects the head, we think of this as that which guards our minds against intellectual attacks on God's word. We are constantly bombarded by the high sounding pronouncements of higher criticism, by the pompous declarations of liberal theology, by supposed proofs that the Bible contains error. Our minds need to be protected at all times.

The original sin on earth came as a result of a

suggestion planted in Eve's mind by the serpent, and Paul was afraid that the same thing might happen to the Corinthians. "But I fear, lest somehow, as the serpent deceived Eve by his craftiness, so your minds may be corrupted from the simplicity that is in Christ" (2 Cor 11:3).

Paul's defence against such attacks is found in 2 Cor 10:5: "Casting down arguments and every high thing that exalts itself against the knowledge of God, bringing every thought into captivity to the obedience of Christ." This means that we judge every human reasoning, speculation, and philosophy by whether it agrees with the teachings of the Lord. If it doesn't, we reject it out of hand.

But the helmet of salvation may have an additional meaning. In 1 Thess 5:8, we are urged to put on the helmet of the *hope of salvation.* The hope of salvation looks forward to the time when our warfare will be ended, and we will be safely home on the shores of Immanuel's Land. How does the Christian put on this helmet? Well, there are times when the battle seems to be going against us. The enemy seems to have the upper hand. Some of our prominent leaders have fallen. Many of the troops began well, but now they have deserted. Others are so entangled in the affairs of this life that they don't have time for active combat. The hosts of hell seem to be advancing while God's cause is languishing. When all the news bulletins are gloomy, it is important to wear the helmet of the hope of salvation. This enables us to say, "The waves may be against us, but the tide is sure to win. Eventually the victory will be ours. God's cause will triumph."

The Sword of the Spirit

The last piece of armour is the sword of the Spirit, which is the word of God (v.17b). W. E. Vine helpfully explains this as follows: "Here the reference is not to the whole Bible as such, but to the individual Scripture which the Spirit brings to our remembrance for use at the appropriate time: a prerequisite being the regular storing of the mind with Scripture."

The classic use of the sword of the Spirit is our Lord's use of the Word in repulsing the temptations of the devil. He did not quote verses at random, but selected the ones that exactly met the need of the moment. Three times He said, "It is written," then used Spirit-given passages that forbade yielding to Satan's evil solicitations.

In order for the Holy Spirit to give us the right verse at the right time, we must have previously memorised or at least known that verse. This emphasizes the importance of Scripture memorisation. When a college student confided in a friend that his professors were gradually eroding his faith, the friend said, "Cease, my son, to hear the instruction that causeth to err from the words of knowledge." The friend couldn't have used the sword of the Spirit in this way if he had not previously memorised Prov 19:27 (AV).

Prayer

Immediately following the six pieces of armour is a

clarion call for prayer. We need not think of prayer as part of the armour, but certainly it is a soldier's vital communication line with headquarters. It is the atmosphere in which the soldier lives and fights. Through prayer he learns God's plan of the day. Through prayer he summons the unseen hosts of the Lord as reinforcements (2 Kings 6:17). Through prayer he wins the victory.

Prayer must be continual, not sporadic.

We must use all kinds of prayer: intercession, supplication, confession, petition – and all mixed with thanksgiving.

It must be in the Spirit, that is, inspired by Him, led by Him, and in accordance with His will.

There must be vigilance in prayer ("being watchful to this end") and perseverance (we must keep on asking, seeking, knocking).

And we must pray for all saints, because we are all in the battle together.

Conclusion

It has often been pointed out that in equipping the christian soldier, God has made no provision for protecting his back. In other words, there must be no retreat. God's soldier must never turn his back and run. When Napoleon's men were being crushed in hand-to-hand combat, he ordered the drummer to beat retreat. The drummer said, "Sir, you never taught me how to beat retreat." The words fired Napoleon with new determination and he went on to win a spectacular victory.

But while there is no retreat for the Christian,

there are times when he should flee. He should flee fornication, that is, any form of sexual immorality (1 Cor 6:18). He should flee from idolatry – not only from graven images, but from anyone and anything that takes the Lord's place in his heart and life (1 Cor 10:14). He should flee from covetousness, the love of money, the desire to be rich (1 Tim 6:11). He should flee youthful lusts, which war against the soul (2 Tim 2:22). Flight, in such cases, is neither cowardice, disgrace, nor defeat. It is the way to remain in the conflict in top fighting condition.

We are in this battle together. Let us remain united and let us pray for one another that we will carry on faithfully to the end and not become casualties. When a missionary fell into sin and had to leave the field, a friend confided to another, "I'm ashamed to admit I never prayed for him. I never thought he would ever need to be kept from this type of sin." We all need prayer. It could happen to any one of us. We are all in danger of making shipwreck of the faith.

John Dorsey described the believer's defence against the devil's tactics in this way:

> I had a battle fierce today within my place of prayer;
> I went to meet and talk with God, but I found Satan there.
> He whispered, "You can't really pray, you lost out long ago;
> You might say some words while on your knees, but you can't pray, you know."
> So then I pulled my helmet down, way down upon my ears,

And found it helped to still his voice and helped
    allay my fears.
I checked my other armour o'er; my feet in peace
    were shod;
My loins with truth were girded 'round; my
    sword the word of God.
My righteous breastplate still was on, my
    heart's love to protect.
My shield of faith was all intact – his fiery darts
    bounced back.
I called on God in Jesus' name, I pled the
    precious blood –
While Satan sneaked away in shame, I met and
    talked with God.

From what we have said so far, it should be clear
that while God is the Teacher in the school of holiness, we have to do our homework. What is true of
prayer is also true of sanctification: without God, we
cannot; without us, God will not. More on that in the
next chapter.

CHAPTER 7

God's Part – Our Part

IN THE area of holiness, there is a mysterious mingling of the divine and the human. God wants all of us to be holy. Only He can make us holy. And He will give us the necessary power. But He will not do it without our participation.

We have to put ourselves in the way of the blessing.

> It is a mistake to look for holiness to visit us as a kind of benign magic, or to expect God's help to come as a windfall apart from conditions known and met. There are plainly marked paths which lead straight to the green pastures; let us walk in them. To desire holiness, for instance, and at the same time to neglect prayer and devotion is to wish one way and walk another.

It is misleading to tell Christians that holiness is by faith alone. It creates the impression that they can sit back and become Christlike without any exertion on their part. It blithely overlooks the hundreds of exhortations in the NT directed to their will and calling for their obedience.

It is equally misleading to teach that the life of victory is found in answering an "altar call". No one denies that a person may truly rededicate his life to the Lord in such an experience. But it is not the be-all and end-all. In fact, its value and significance will quickly fade unless it is followed up by diligent exertion.

So we must beware of neat slogans such as "Let go and let God," "Believe the promise; receive the filling," or "Stop trying and start trusting." As Donald Campbell says, "The Spirit does not operate automatically in a believer's life. He waits to be depended on."

No Instant Holiness

God has not seen fit to dispense holiness pills which, like a divine antibiotic, will solve the problem once for all. He has not given a quick fix or a shortcut to holiness. Rather He has prescribed a lifetime process in which He provides the power and calls on us to appropriate it day by day.

Salvation is by faith alone, but holiness is by faith and works.

Every one of us is in need of being changed. Whether we are grumpy, nervously irritable, quick-tempered, impatient, tactless, unloving, thin-skinned, self-centred, deceitful, whether we use minced oaths or private profanity, or whether we have habits that are not Christ-honouring, we need to be changed. The Lord can produce the change. In fact, He is waiting to do it. But He is also waiting for our co-operation.

His method to achieve our cooperation is to put us under grace and not under law. The believer desires to be holy because of love to the Saviour and not because of fear of punishment. This is the next subject which we will cover.

CHAPTER 8

How To Make Men Holy!

THE QUESTION is, "Once a person is saved, how can we be sure that he will live a holy life? What is the best method to insure that he will walk in separation from sin and the world?"

If the responsibility of devising a programme were left to man, he would almost certainly resort to a system of rules and regulations. He would insist that you must put a Christian under law. By achieving certain standards of behaviour, the believer would become holy. This do and you will live.

This is holiness by law-keeping. The laws might include the Ten Commandments, Sabbath-observance, prohibition of alcohol, drugs, movies, tobacco, dancing, immorality, etc. The possible number of do's and dont's is legion.

But since law without punishment is only good advice, there must be a penalty for those who fail to live up to the code. And the most general punishment prescribed is the loss of salvation. In other words, we are saved by faith, but if we do not live the christian life, we will forfeit eternal life. Those who advocate salvation by law-keeping in one form or another sincerely believe that the only thing that will keep believers on the straight and narrow is the fear of punishment.

This approach to holiness is fatally defective. It is

not scriptural. Nowhere does the Bible suggest that we can become holy by obeying certain laws or avoiding certain taboos. On the contrary, Paul rebuked the Galatians for even entertaining such a notion. He asked, "Are you so foolish? Having begun in the Spirit, are you now being made perfect by the flesh?" (Gal 3:3). In other words, if you couldn't be saved by law-keeping in the first place, how could you ever become holy by that method?"

Not only is this approach to holiness unscriptural – it doesn't work! As James Denney has said, "it is not Mount Sinai but Mount Calvary that produces saints." The law demands strength from one who has none, does not provide the power, and curses him if he can't display it. Also, under law sin is aroused (Rom 7:8-13). Because of his fallen human nature, a person wants to do what is forbidden. It is not the law's fault, but indwelling sin in mankind.

God's Way of Holiness

God's way of holiness is different. It is by grace, not by law. The Lord says, in effect, "I have saved you by my grace. Now out of love, not fear, go out and live in a manner that is consistent with this. I have given you the indwelling Holy Spirit and He will empower you to walk worthy of your calling. And I will reward you every time you resist temptation, every time you say no to sin."

Of course, the question naturally arises, "How do I know what kind of behaviour is consistent with the Christian calling?" So God says to us, "All right, I have filled the NT with practical instructions in righteousness for you. Some of these instructions are even called commandments, but just remember that they are not laws with penalties attached. Rather they are specific examples of the lifestyle that pleases Me."

The moment we are saved, we are given a position of holiness before God. Because we are in Christ, we have a holy standing. Our responsibility is to see that our practice corresponds to our position, our state to our standing.

Love, not Fear

Under grace the motive for holiness is love, not fear. Believers instinctively want to be holy when they remember the price the Lord Jesus paid to put away their sins. The memory of Calvary is the strongest possible impetus to live soberly, righteously, and godly. The believer asks, then quickly answers:

> Need I that a law should bind me
> Captive unto Thee?
> Captive is my heart, rejoicing
> Never to be free.

Someone may object, "If you just put Christians under grace, then they will go out and do anything they want and live any way they please." In other words, the doctrine of grace encourages sin. Spurgeon answered:

> It is neither according to nature or to grace for men to find an argument for sin in the goodness of God ... Shall I hate God because He is kind to me?

> Shall I curse Him because He blesses me? ... The
> believer in Jesus reasons in quite a different
> fashion. Is God so good? – then I will not grieve
> Him. Is He so ready to forgive my transgressions?
> – then I will love Him and offend no more ... We
> need no nobler or more cogent arguments to lead a
> man to thorough consecration to God's cause and
> detestation of all evil than those fetched from the
> free grace of God.

It is true that grace, like everything else, can be
abused. Undoubtedly some have used their freedom
from the law as a pretext for sinning. But these are
exceptions.

It is true that we are free from the law, but we are
not lawless. Rather, as Paul points out in 1
Cor 9:21, we are under law to Christ. The Lord Jesus
and not the law is the believer's rule of life.

It is true that we do anything we want, but only in
the sense that what we want is now different. We
want to be holy. We want to resist temptation, to flee
from it. We want to do the thing that pleases the
heart of Christ. Only in that sense do we live the way
we please.

We do not deny that there are Christians who live
saintly lives in every segment of the Church today.
But some do so because they are properly grounded
in the grace of God. Others do it in spite of their
legalistic orientation.

Now we must pause to consider a question that
inevitably arises. Is it possible for a believer to achieve
perfect holiness, to reach the place where he no
longer sins? What do the Scriptures say?

CHAPTER 9

Principles of Christian Conduct

THE QUESTION is, "What is appropriate behaviour for a believer? What may he do, and what should he not do? Is this activity right or wrong?"

The Bible gives us a general outline as to how a believer can walk worthy of his heavenly calling. It answers many questions so directly that there is no need to look further. For instance, it teaches that it is never right to become involved in an unequal yoke (2 Cor 6:14). A believer must not marry an unbeliever, enter a business partnership with an unbeliever, or engage in christian service with an unbeliever. There is no need to pray about it, or seek counsel. The answer is already there in God's word.

But there are hundreds of situations that arise in the christian life that are not dealt with directly in the Scriptures. If the Bible took up every problem area, it would be so massive that we wouldn't be able to carry it around!

So what God has done is this. He has given us a set of principles. When the question arises, "Is it all right for me to do this?" we apply the principles one by one. I cannot think of any problem that couldn't be solved by using this method. It's like feeding a problem into a computer, pushing the appropriate controls, and finding the answer staring at us. Here are the principles, in the form of questions.

Is There Any Glory for God in It?

We always ask, "Is there any harm in it?" But we should also ask "Is there any glory for God in it?" The apostle Paul lays down the principle that whatever we do, we should do to the glory of God, and this applies to such common activities as eating and drinking (1 Cor 10:31). A famous evangelist preaches the gospel to the glory of God, and his wife washes dishes with the same motive. Over her kitchen sink is a printed reminder: "Divine services conducted here three times daily."

Any honourable work can be done to the glory of God. Even christian slaves working in the field can serve "as to Christ," "as servants of Christ," "as to the Lord, and not to men" (Eph 6:5-7).

But there are many things in which there is no glory for God, that is, things that are dishonest, impure, unrighteous, or even questionable. Before engaging in these things, it would be ridiculous to bow the head and pray, "Lord Jesus, be glorified in what I am about to do."

Is It "of the World"?

The world of unregenerate people has its own lifestyle, fashions, music, art, religion, philosophy. It appeals to the body rather than the spirit, to man's depraved nature rather than to what Christ has ordained for him.

Believers are not of the world any more than Christ is of the world (John 17:16). Because the world is still hostile to God, anyone who loves the world is His enemy (James 4:4; 1 John 2:15).

When a person is born again, he receives a Spirit-given intuition as to what is worldly. And as he grows in grace, that intuition may become keener. A believer ordered a state-of-the-art television set. When the delivery truck arrived, he looked out of his window and saw this advertisement on the side: "Brings the world into your living room." That was enough! He told the driver to take the TV set back.

Would Jesus Have Done It?

The Saviour left us an example that we should follow His steps (1 Pet 2:21). So it is valid to apply this test to any area of behaviour: What would Jesus do?

Years ago, Charles Sheldon wrote a book called *In His Steps,* in which a christian congregation decided to apply this test in daily life. The result was that the community was revolutionised.

Someone may remind us that Jesus ate with publicans and sinners (Mark 2:15, 16). That is true, but it is also true that He was always faithful to God His Father when He did so. He never condoned their sins, or compromised His own testimony. We too may eat with the ungodly sinners if we reprove their sins (Eph 5:11b), and share the gospel with them (Rom 1:14). "The example of Christ in His walk on earth should ever be before us as the only standard of holiness" (R.C. Chapman).

Would You Like to Be Found Doing It When Jesus Returns?

No one knows the time of the Saviour's return. It

could happen at any moment. The apostle John reminds us of the possibility of shame at His coming (1 John 2:28). We would be ashamed if He found us in evil or even questionable activities, watching suggestive movies, reading smutty literature, indulging our fleshly appetites. We would be ashamed if He had to say to us, "What are you doing here?" Or if He had to ask us, as He asked backslidden Peter, "Do you love Me more than these?"

The hope of Christ's imminent return exerts a purifying influence on a believer's life (1 John 3:3). But it is not enough to hold the truth intellectually; the truth must hold us practically. Those who love His appearing (2 Tim. 4:8) are those whose lives are moulded by the blessed hope.

Which Nature Does It Feed?

In another chapter, we take up the subject of the two natures in depth. It is enough here to summarize. Every believer has two natures – an old one and a new one. The old nature is incurably evil; the new nature is indescribably good. These natures are constantly warring against each other. The nature we feed is the nature that wins.

We feed the natures by what we see, hear, and do; by where we go; by the company we keep; by the thought-life we encourage. If we feed the wolf within, we can't expect the lamb to win.

Can You Feel Free to Do It When You Remember that Your Body Is the Temple of the Holy Spirit?

The moment a person is saved, the Holy Spirit takes up permanent residence in his body (1 Cor 6:19). The Third Person of the Trinity looks on the body as a temple – a holy place in which to dwell. We are to live in the consciousness that our body is *holy* and that it is indwelt by a *Holy* Person.

As long as we are gripped by this truth, we will resist sexual impurity, gluttony, drunkenness. We will not allow ourselves to become addicted to cancer-producing agents, such as tobacco, or mind-altering drugs. Rather we will follow reasonable rules of health and safety to maintain our body in good health for the Lord's sake.

Is It Fitting Behaviour for a Child of God?

As children of the King, we are expected to walk worthy of our high calling (Eph 5:8b; Col 1:10).

A story is told (it may only be a story) about the son of King Louis XVI of France. When an evil woman tried to corrupt him into speaking vile language, the little prince would clench his fists, stamp his feet and say, "I will not say it, I will not say those filthy words. I was born to be a king, and I won't talk that way!"

When we find a person from the slums wallowing in the gutter, we may be grieved but not surprised. But when we see the ruler's son living as a derelict on skid row, we are shocked. We don't expect that from a son of a president.

People of the world expect better conduct of believers than they do of themselves. When a believer slips, they pounce on him, "Oh! I thought you were a

Christian!" No mention of the fact that they commit the same sin habitually!

But that is the way it should be. The world should expect more from us, and they should get it.

If It Involves the Expenditure of Money, Could the Money Be Better Spent?

Some things in life are good; some are better; some are best of all. We constantly have to make value judgments in order to maximise our effectiveness.

The good is often the enemy of the best. We may spend money on things that may not be sinful, yet they may be trivial, transient, and non-essential. On the other hand, we may use our money in the spread of the gospel, thus ensuring ourselves a welcoming committee at the gates of glory (Luke 16:9).

This principle is not intended to put a guilt-trip on people over every pound they spend. But it should open to them the thrilling possibility of using funds in such a way that a work will be done for God that will last for all eternity.

Could the Time Be Better Spent?

Once again, the use of our time should not be a matter of legal bondage but of glorious liberty. We are all entrusted with twenty-four hours every day, and we decide how it is to be spent. It has endless possibilities for good, for evil – and for waste.

As good stewards, we are to redeem the time (Eph 5:16), that is, make the most of every opportunity. This will inevitably mean dropping many activities for those with a higher priority. It may mean refusing invitations. It may mean cutting down on hours of employment in order to give oneself to prayer and the ministry of the Word. It should mean giving precedence to meetings of the assembly over family gatherings and other social engagements.

Faithfulness in making these decisions leads to wider spheres of service.

What Effect Will Your Conduct Have on Others?

There are certain activities in life that are morally neutral. They are called matters of moral indifference. A Christian has the right to do them. They are not wrong in themselves.

But these actions become wrong if they stumble or offend another brother. Notice how Paul deals with the subject in Rom 14:

> ... resolve this, not to put a stumbling-block or a cause to fall in our brothers's way (v.13b).
> ... if your brother is grieved because of your food, you are no longer walking in love. Do not destroy with your food the one for whom Christ died (v. 15).
> ... do not destroy the work of God for the sake of food (v. 20a).

And again in 1 Cor 8:9-13 the apostle says:

> But beware lest somehow this liberty of yours becomes a stumbling block to those who are weak. For if anyone sees you who have knowledge eating in an idol's temple, will not the conscience of him

> who is weak be emboldened to eat those things
> offered to idols?
> And because of your knowledge shall the weak
> brother perish, for whom Christ died?
> But when you thus sin against the brethren, and
> wound their weak conscience, you sin against
> Christ.
> Therefore if food makes my brother stumble, I will
> never again eat meat, lest I make my brother
> stumble.

When Paul says "All things are lawful for me, but
all things do not edify" (1 Cor 10:23b), the primary
thought is not so much a matter of self-edification as
of edifying others.

> The guiding principle for us all towards others is
> that we may be a means of edifying them, that is,
> of building them up spiritually. A freedom which
> is enjoyed at the expense of detriment to others
> cannot be really beneficial to oneself (W.E. Vine).

So although a Christian may have the right to eat
pork or shellfish or drink wine in moderation, he has
the greater right to renounce that liberty rather
than grieve a brother in the Lord.

It is well known that Charles Haddon Spurgeon
was a smoker. He defended the habit, even though
he was one of God's greatest gifts to the Church.
There is a story that one day he saw on a billboard,
"Smoke the tobacco that Spurgeon smokes."That was
all he needed to drop the habit.

Is It Doubtful?
"Whatever is not from faith is sin" (Rom 14:23).

This is still speaking about matters of moral indifference, things that are not intrinsically wrong. If I think a certain thing is wrong, and I go ahead and do it anyway, then I have sinned. It may not be wrong for another Christian; he may have perfect liberty to do it. But if my conscience is not clear, if I cannot do it with faith or with the confidence that it is legitimate, then I sin when I do it.

Sometimes when it is hard to tell if the laundry is white or tell-tale gray, the rule to follow is, "If it's doubtful, it's dirty." Adapt the rule to matters of moral indifference – "If it's doubtful, it's wrong to do it."

Does It Have the Appearance of Evil?

1 Thess 5:22 reads in the original Authorised Version, "Abstain from all appearance of evil." Though the modern versions uniformly direct us to abstain from *every form* of evil, the older reading is not unbiblical and carries a needed warning. An unmarried couple may drive across the country together and be perfectly innocent of immorality, but it leaves them open to suspicion. A Sunday School teacher may go into a bar for a Coke, but it may be hard to convince one of his students who happens to walk by just as he emerges.

Is It a Weight?

There is a difference between a sin and a weight. A sin is always wrong; a weight may not be wrong but it is a hindrance. We should "lay aside every weight and ... run with endurance the race that is set before us" (Heb 12:1). In the Olympic races there are rules that must be observed; if they are not followed, the runner is disqualified. Now there is nothing in the rules to prevent a runner from wearing two-pound ankle weights. He can wear them but he won't win the race.

Paul was thinking of weights when he wrote, "All things are lawful for me, but all things are not helpful (1 Cor 6:12a; 10:33a). They are not conducive to making progress for Christ. They are not necessarily wrong but they might not be profitable.

What is a weight in the Christian race? An unspiritual friendship, a time-consuming job, an overly-absorbing hobby, a monopolising sport, indiscriminate and inordinate TV viewing ... all these could hinder a believer in winning the prize. In fact, excessive time spent in any subordinate activity could become a weight.

Is It Enslaving?

There is another area where something may be quite legitimate but it must be avoided if it is addictive. The apostle said, "All things are lawful for me, but I will not be brought under the power of any" (1 Cor 6:12b). He is speaking of areas that are not distinctly wrong in themselves, but they become wrong if they hold us in their power. Paul would not allow himself to become addicted to foods or beverages. We might add to the list drugs, sports and TV.

How Does It Appear in the Eyes of Christ?

Someone suggested that the greatest test for Christian behaviour is how it appears in the eyes of Christ. Does He approve? Would we be embarrassed to have Him sitting beside us?

The truth is that He is present with us at all times. As the old spiritual says, "Oh, He sees all we do, He hears all we say, my Lord is a-writin' all the time."

Constant remembrance that the holy Saviour is our Companion at all times is bound to have a sanctifying influence on our lives.

These then are principles that God has given to guide us in our moral decision-making. As we know them, remember them, and apply them, we are assured of making the choices that will please His heart and keep us on the highway to holiness.

Unfortunately most of us experience wild swings in our lives. We alternate between victory and defeat. What we want is deliverance from the power of indwelling sin. We want continuous revival. There is a way to find it.

CHAPTER 10

Let's Get the Facts Straight

THERE ARE several truths that will be especially helpful to us in seeking deliverance from the power of indwelling sin. Let us look at them.

The Two Natures

We should know that every Christian has two natures (Rom. 7:14-25). One is the old, evil, corrupt nature with which he was born. The other is the new, pure, holy nature which he received at the time of his conversion. We might call them the Adam nature and the Christ nature. One Christian put it this way: "Sin was taken out of my heart, but my grandfather is still in my bones."

The old nature is totally bad. Paul's experience is ours as well; he said, "For I know that in me (that is, in my flesh) nothing good dwells" (Rom 7:18a). Therefore we should never look for anything good in our old nature and never be surprised or disappointed when we don't find it. It is not only *totally* bad; it is *incurably* bad! It is no better after a long life of holy living than it was when that life began. In fact, God is not in the business of improving the old nature. He condemned it at the Cross of Calvary, and wants us to be dead to its attempts to run our lives.

Paul likened the old nature to a dead body that was strapped to his back. (Obviously the corpse was decaying and stinking.) It went with him wherever he went causing him to cry out in anguish, "O wretched man that I am! Who will deliver me from this body of death?"

The new nature is the life of Christ and it is therefore totally good and capable only of good. It is pure, noble, righteous, lovely, and true. All its thoughts, desires, motives, and actions are Christlike.

It is not surprising that two such opposite natures are in constant conflict. (They could hardly live together peaceably, could they?) This conflict begins at conversion. The new believer experiences an inward struggle that he never had before. The old nature seeks to pull him down, like the law of gravity, whereas the new nature seeks to elevate him to greater heights of holiness. The warfare is so intense that he is often tempted to doubt his salvation. But he should not doubt. The very fact that he has this conflict is a sign that he is saved. He wouldn't have it if he didn't possess two natures.

The conflict of the two natures has been compared to Rebekah's experience when she felt twins struggling in her womb and cried "Why am I this way?" What happened in the womb of Rebekah happens in the heart of every true child of God who seeks to go forward with Him:

> When conscious of the presence of the Spirit, we also become conscious of the traitor within. The young Christian is inclined to cry, "Why am I this way?" The older brother, the flesh, wants his way. The younger brother, the Spirit, is quiet and restful, seemingly unable to prevail. But with us,

as with Rebekah's children, the elder shall serve the younger. For God has promised blessing on all that comes from the Spirit, never on what comes of the flesh (Barnhouse).

The battle that began at conversion continues through all of life. It is a war in which there is no discharge except through death or the Rapture. But the good news is that we will be freed from the old nature the moment we see the Saviour, for to see Him is to be like Him.

It is important to realise that every child of God has this conflict. Paul reminds us that no temptation has overtaken us except such as is *common to man* (1 Cor 10:13). Young people wrestling with youthful lusts are apt to think that older people, or preachers, or missionaries are exempt from dark passions and fiery temptations. Nonsense! Just as Rebekah had two babies struggling within her (Gen 25:22, 23), so every believer has two natures struggling within him.

The old nature feeds on whatever is unclean, while the new nature hungers for that which is pure and holy. They are like the raven and the dove that Noah released from the ark. The unclean raven fed on all the floating carrion and garbage. But the dove returned to the ark until it could find a clean place to land and feed (Gen 8:6-12). So the old nature loves to feed on Hollywood lust and TV filth. But the new nature loves the sincere milk of the word of God. The importance of this lies in the fact that the nature we feed is the nature that wins. A man was complaining that his two dogs were always fighting. When his friend asked, "Which dog wins?" he answered, "The one I say 'get 'im' to". That's the way it is with the two natures. The one to which we say " get 'im" to is the one that wins. This is also illustrated in the case of the cuckoo. It lays an egg in another bird's nest then lets the other bird hatch it along with its own. When the mother bird brings food to the nest, she finds open beaks waiting for her. Everything depends on which birds get the food. If the young cuckoo succeeds, it soon pushes the other birds out of the nest. So it is in the nest of our life.

It was My Old Nature that Did It

We mustn't excuse our sinning by passing the buck to the old nature. That is a form of blame-shifting that will not work. God holds the *person* responsible, not the nature. Perhaps you've heard the fictitious story of the speeder who said to the judge, "Your honour, it was my old nature that was speeding." To which the judge replied, "I fine your old nature £50 for speeding, and I fine your new nature £50 for being an accessory before the fact." Blaming the old nature just isn't the way to go.

Acts of Sin v. the Practice of Sin

Another truth we should know is that there is a difference between committing acts of sin and being ruled by sin. Every Christian commits acts of sin even though his life isn't dominated by it. He is not *sinless,* but he does *sin less.*

In his first epistle, John makes it clear that believers do sin. He says that if we deny that, we deceive ourselves and make God a liar (1:8-10). But he goes on to say: "No one who abides in Him practises sin. No one who practises sin has either seen Him or known Him. The one who goes on sinning is of the devil; for the devil has sinned from the beginning. No one who is born of God practices sin, because His seed abides in him, and he cannot go on sinning, because he is born of God" (3:6, 8a, 9). The fact that John is speaking about the practice of sin is supported by his assertion that the devil has sinned from the beginning (3:8); it has been his characteristic behaviour. But believers are not of the devil; their lives are not characterized by sin.

This raises the question, "When does the committing of sin become the practice of sin?" The Bible does not answer the question. If it did, we would push permissiveness to the limit. So the silence of the Word serves as a healthful warning against sinning at all.

Is Sinless Perfection Possible?

There are some who sincerely believe that it is possible for a Christian to reach the place where he no longer sins, where he has achieved entire sanctification. They contend that through a crisis experience of the Holy Spirit, usually after conversion, the sin nature is eradicated. From that time on they no longer sin.

People who claim this just don't understand what sin is. It is any act, thought, or word that comes short of God's perfection (Rom 3:23). It is lawlessness, that is, the determination to have one's own way (1 John

3:4). It is not only doing wrong, but failing to do what is right (James 4:17). It is doing anything that one's conscience condemns (Rom 14:23). "Sin pollutes the best thing the believer does. It mars his repentance. There is filth in his tears and unbelief in his faith." One spiritual saint said that even his repentance needed to be cleansed by the blood of Christ. Another, who realised that everything he did was stained by sin, wrote:

> The holiest hours we spend
>   In prayer upon our knees,
> The times when most we think
>   Our songs of praise will please,
> Thou Searcher of all hearts,
>   Forgiveness pour on these.

"The true Christian is not one who has lost his ability to sin, but his desire and willingness." He now hates sin. He is ashamed when he does sin, and is smitten with a feeling of uncleanness.

But someone may ask. "If a Christian cannot be sinless, why does it say in 1 John 2:1, 'My little children, these things I write to you, that you may not sin.'" The answer is that God's standard is always perfection. A holy God cannot condone any sin. He could not say, for example, "Sin as little as possible." That would be approving sin and God cannot do that. So His standard for His people is perfection. But He immediately makes provision for failure. In the same verse, He goes on to say, "And if anyone sins, we have an Advocate with the Father, Jesus Christ the righteous." And in the previous chapter, He had already insisted that Christians do sin. Note:

> If we say we have no sin, we deceive ourselves,
> and the truth is not in us (1:8).
> If we say we have not sinned, we make Him
> a liar, and His word is not in us (1:10).

It is true that there are verses that seem to say that a believer can be sinless. First, Rom 6:2 says that the believer has died to sin. This refers to his position. God sees him as having died with Christ. The old man was crucified with Him. But in v. 11, Paul says that we should reckon ourselves to be dead to sin; that is our everyday practice. If v. 2 meant that we were sinless, then the exhortation of verse 11 would be unnecessary.

Three other verses speak of the believer as having been set free from sin (Rom 6:7, 18, 22). In all these verses, the apostle is using the illustration of slaves and masters. Before we were saved we were slaves of sin. In the death of Christ, we died to sin *as master*. We have been set free from sin's dominion and have become slaves of righteousness and of God.

Then there are several verses in the NT using the words *perfect, perfected, and perfection* that might suggest sinlessness to the casual reader (Matt 5:48; Phil 3:12; Phil 3:15 AV; 2 Tim 3:16, 17 AV; Heb 6:1; 9:9; 10:14; 13:20, 21 AV; James 3:2b; Rev 3:1, 2).

Generally speaking the word *perfect* means complete, full-grown or mature. When applied to Christians still living on earth, it never means sinless. In Heb 9:9, it refers to a perfect conscience, in Heb

10:14, it refers to a perfect standing before God.

Another verse that has been used to teach sinless perfection is 1 Thess 5:23. But here Paul is praying that sanctification would extend to every part of the believer's being – spirit, soul, and body – so that he would be without blame at the Lord's coming.

Then, of course, there are those unsettling verses in John's first epistle (3:6, 9; 5:18). As already explained, these verses are talking about habitual behaviour. The verbs are in the present continuous tense. The person who has been born of God does not practise sin. He does not live in sin. Sin does not characterise his life.

But is the teaching of sinless perfection serious? Any doctrine that is contrary to the word of God is serious. Many earnest, sincere believers who have strived for sinless perfection have ended up disillusioned, and, in many cases, have suffered from depression and mental breakdowns. In his book *Holiness, the False and the True,* H.A. Ironside tells of his own futile search for entire sanctification, of his emotional breakdown, and of the peace that came to his life when he was introduced to the true doctrine of christian holiness.

I Can't Help It – I Have to Sin

We must not say that we have to sin. It never says that in the Bible and it isn't true. If we say we have to sin, we are saying, in effect, that the Holy Spirit isn't powerful enough to enable us to resist temptation. But He is. The trouble is not with Him but with ourselves. We sin when we do not appropriate His power. We sin when we want to.

> To say that I must sin, is to deny the foundations of Christianity, for sin shall not have dominion over the believer (Rom 6:14); to say that I cannot sin, is to deceive myself (1 John 1:8) to say that I need not sin, is to declare a divine principle, for the law of the Spirit of life in Christ makes me free from the law of sin (Rom 8:2). Thanks be unto God which gives us the victory!

Relationship and Fellowship

When a Christian sins, he doesn't lose his salvation but he does lose the *joy* of his salvation. Fellowship in the family of God is broken but relationship with God is not broken. Through the new birth, he became a child of God, and nothing can ever change that. But when he sins, his fellowship with God is broken, because "God is light and in Him is no darkness at all" (1 John 1:5). The happy family spirit remains broken until the sin is confessed and forsaken (1 John 1:9; Prov 28:13).

Is Any Sin Unconquerable?

The believer should know that there is deliverance from any sin that he may commit (1 Cor 10:13). We all have some besetting sin or sins, some unwelcome intruder that seems to hold us in its grip; some habit that pins us down. How often we despair of ever getting complete and final freedom! The truth is that both the Word and human experience show that no case is too hard for God, no sin is greater than His power.

Not an Act But a Process

But it is equally important to know that there is no single experience that will give us once-for-all deliverance from the power of indwelling sin. Unfortunately this fact is often denied in the Church today. Preachers often offer the people a shortcut to holiness. In a climactic "altar call", they encourage their listeners to come forward to receive the filling, the baptism, or the life of victory. The people are deluded if they think that such a crisis experience will automatically and permanently catapult them to a higher plateau of holiness.

Deliverance is a moment-by-moment process – not an instantaneous achievement. The promise is "As your days, so shall your strength be" (Deut 33:25). When we are told to "be filled with the Spirit" (Eph 5:18), the literal meaning is "be continually being filled with the Spirit." It is a present, continuous action. No "altar" experience that we may have had last night will guarantee deliverance when today's temptations arise.

The Wilful Sin

Some believers suffer needless anxiety that they have committed the wilful sin of Heb 10:26, 27. They reason that since their will is involved when they do sin, therefore they are guilty of the wilful sin and are doomed to the judgment and fiery indignation which will devour God's adversaries. But that is simply not true. It is essential for us to realise that there is a difference between acts of sin and the wilful sin of Heb 10. The wilful sin is apostasy. It is defined in v.

29 as trampling underfoot the Son of God, counting the blood of the covenant by which he was sanctified a common thing, and insulting the Spirit of grace. No true believer can ever be guilty of that! The very fact that a person worries that he has committed this sin is an indication that he has not. Those who apostatise from the christian faith are so hardened and arrogant that they never give it a second thought. They have no fear of God or of His punishment.

Non-Helps to Victory

Before we leave the list of things we should know, it is helpful to remind ourselves that there are certain attitudes and actions that do not help us in the quest for holiness. *Asceticism* does not help. In Col 2:23 Paul says that while self-torture and self-denial may give the appearance of godliness, they are "of no value against the indulgence of the flesh." *Monasticism* does not help. A person may separate himself from the world in a monastery cell, but he cannot separate himself from his own nature. *Introspection* doesn't help. There is no victory in self; occupation with self is like casting your anchor inside the boat. *Passivity* is not the answer. Holiness doesn't descend on those who idly wait for it. Neither does it come through *an intensive study of temptation*. The more we think about temptation, the more likely we are to yield. Finally, victory doesn't come through *giving up in despair*. That is defeat, and God cannot use defeated Christians.

So much for things we should know. Now let us move on to action that we must take.

CHAPTER 11

The Way of Victory – Be Filled with the Spirit

ONLY God can make us holy, but He will not do it without our cooperation. As in so many areas of the christian life, there is a curious mingling of the divine and the human. God provides the power but we must avail ourselves of it. Our obligation is to be filled with the Spirit. It is only as we walk in the Spirit that we will not fulfil the desires of the flesh.

But what does it mean to be filled with the Spirit? This sounds very ethereal and mystical. It sounds like something that is reserved for preachers and missionaries. Not so! It is something that is commanded for all God's people and it does not call for anything that is impossible for any believer. To make it as simple and practical as possible, let us suggest some basic steps that are involved in being filled with the Spirit.

Don't Let Sins Accumulate

In order to keep ourselves clean, we must confess and forsake sin as soon as we are aware of it in our lives (Prov 28:13; 1 John 1:9). All sin should be confessed to God since all sin is against Him. If people have been wronged, then the confession should be made to them also. True confession should be:

75

Immediate – we should not wait until the end of the day or the end of the week.

Unconditional – do not say, "If I have done anything wrong ..." or "I'll forgive you if you forgive me." Don't be like the woman who said, "If I have done anything wrong, I am willing to be forgiven."

Complete – a man confessed that he had stolen a length of rope but neglected to say that there was a horse at the other end of the rope.

Specific – tell it as it is. Call the monster by its right name – drunkenness rather than indiscretion, stealing rather than borrowing. Peter did not say, "I am an inadequate man," but "I am a sinful man, O Lord."

Accompanied by the determination to forsake the sin – this is not confession: "I stole a crate of Bartlett pears, but better make it two. I'm going after the other crate tonight."

Heartfelt – just say it, "I was wrong. I am sorry. Please forgive me."

When we honestly confess our sins, we can know on the authority of the word of God that we have been forgiven. God has promised to forgive if we confess, and He is true to His promise. We appropriate forgiveness by faith.

But someone may say, "I don't feel forgiven". That

may be so, but you are forgiven, whether you feel it or not. Assurance of forgiveness does not come through changeable feelings but through the unchangeable Word.

Someone else may say, "I know that God has forgiven me but I can't forgive myself." Such an attitude is an unnecessary form of self-torture. If God has forgiven us, the matter is settled. Why go on wallowing in guilt?

It is true that when God forgives, He forgets (Heb 10:17). This does not mean that God has a bad memory, but rather that He will never again bring up these sins against us. They are forgotten in the sense that the case is closed. A broken-hearted penitent, who had slipped back into an evil habit, cried out, "O Lord, I confess. I have done it again." The story is that the Lord replied, "What have you done again?" In that split second after he confessed, the Lord had forgotten.

Corrie ten Boom reminds us that God not only forgets – He puts up a NO FISHING sign. He doesn't want us to dredge up our own sins or the sins of others that have been confessed and forgiven. The only way we should ever remember them is as a warning not to commit them again.

It should be added that the circle of our confession should be as wide as the circle of our sin, whether to God alone, or also to some person we have wronged, or even to the entire local church. Leith Samuel helpfully advises, "Where your sin was in thought, let your confession be in thought. Do not go up to some woman and tell her you lusted after her in your

heart, causing embarrassment and confusion and
further sin as happens in some circles ... If it was
secret sin in thought, let it be confessed secretly in
thought, and not publicly where someone else's mind
is going to be smeared and tainted ... What has been
committed openly in the fellowship of the church, let
the fellowship of the church have the apology. Have
you let them down? Tell them you are sorry. Have
you been bitter against them, and they know it,
because of the things you have said? Well, let it be
said also that you are desperately sorry for the things
you have said."

Harry Lloyd became convicted that his friends and
customers were ascribing greater sanctity to him as
a christian businessman than he deserved. It both-
ered him that they praised and admired him as a
shining example of a dedicated Christian, so he wrote
the following disclaimer in a public letter:

> I spend almost all of my energies and priorities in
> forwarding my business and in the pursuit of
> personal pleasure.
> I practically never read the Bible.
> My sins in both thought and deed are grave indeed.
> The 10% I give to God's work is a mockery insofar
> as sacrificial giving is concerned and a pittance of
> what I could give.
> I am demanding and critical as a boss.
> All too often I am harsh and unloving as a husband
> and father.
> I don't attend church without fail like I did as a
> child.
> When people praise me, you can see why I feel like
> such a fraud. That's why I feel compelled to reveal,

with shame, what a miserable example of a Christian I am. Praise no one except ONE."

It is not often that we hear as honest a confession as this, still less frequent that we indulge in it ourselves.

Make Restitution Whenever Possible

The grace of God teaches us that we must make right the wrongs of the past to whatever extent possible. This means restoring to the rightful owner things we have taken wrongly. It might also mean paying interest on money that was stolen.

Zacchaeus is the classic example of this in the NT. After his conversion, he said, "Look, Lord, I give half of my goods to the poor; and if I have taken anything from anyone by false accusation, I restore fourfold" (Luke 19:8). He didn't do this in order to be saved, but because he was saved.

Restitution must be sincere and thorough. We must not be like the man who wrote to the Internal Revenue Service, "I haven't been able to sleep because last year when I filled out my income tax report, I deliberately misrepresented my income. I am enclosing a check for $150, and if I still can't sleep, I'll send you the rest."

There are situations where, because of the passing of time, or because of changed conditions, it is no longer possible to make restitution. The Lord knows about this, and if the sin is confessed, He accepts the sincere desire for the actual fact.

Years ago when W. P. Nicholson was preaching in Belfast, the Spirit of God moved in such power that people began to return tools that they had stolen from the local factories. So many were returned that the companies had to build sheds to hold the tools. Finally, they sent out a notice to the public asking that no more be returned; there was no room!

Similarly, once when F. B. Meyer preached at the Keswick Convention, the local post office was swamped with work as Christians hurried to return borrowed and stolen money and make restitution in other ways.

Present Your Body a Living Sacrifice

We move on to a third action we must take in order to know practical holiness. We must yield ourselves to the Lord, and our members as instruments of righteousness (Rom 12:1, 2; 6:19). Yielding begins as a crisis but must continue as a process. There must be a first time when we present our bodies as a living sacrifice to the Lord. But then day by day, moment by moment, we must accept His will in place of our own. We must turn over the controls to Him. We must deny self, take up the cross, and follow Him. Just as confession keeps us clean, so yielding keeps us available.

Anne Grannis has captured the real meaning of consecration in the following lines:

> I want my life so cleared of self that my dear Lord may come
> And set up His own furnishings and make my heart his home;
> And since I know what this requires, each morning while it's still,

I slip into the secret place and leave with Him –
my will.
He always takes it graciously, presenting me with
His.
I'm ready then to start the day and any task there
is.
And this is how my Lord controls my interests, my
ills,
Because we meet at break of day for an exchange
of wills.

When Bishop Taylor Smith used to get out of bed
in the morning, he would kneel by that bed, and
every morning he said these simple words, "Lord, my
bed Thine altar, myself Thy living sacrifice." He was
daily placed at the Lord's disposal.

When Arthur Pierson asked George Muller, "What
is the secret of the great work and the wonderful
things that God has done through you?", Mr Muller
looked up for a moment, then bowed his head lower
and lower until it was almost between his knees. He
was silent for a moment or two and then said, "Many
years ago there came a day in my life when George
Muller died. As a young man, I had a great many
ambitions, but there came a day when I died to all
those things, and I said, 'Henceforth, Lord Jesus, not
my will but Thine,' and from that day God began to
work in and through me."

General Booth expressed it in a different way. He
said, "When I was a lad of seventeen, I determined
that God should have all there was of William Booth."

Saturate Your Life With the Word

A fourth absolute necessity is staying close to the

Word, so close that our lives are saturated by it. This means reading, memorising, studying, meditating on, and obeying the word of God. By reading the Word, we learn the general outline of God's behaviour code for us. By memorising it, we enable the Holy Spirit to remind us of appropriate passages in times of witness, temptation, or indecision. By studying it, we are delivered from false doctrines and false expectations. By meditating on it, we are changed by beholding the One of whom it speaks. And by obeying it, we are led in paths of righteousness.

The psalmist recognised the link between sanctification and the Word; he wrote: "How can a young man cleanse his way? By taking heed according to Thy word ... Thy word have I hidden in my heart, that I might not sin against Thee" (Ps 119:9, 11). Jesus confirmed the link when He prayed, "Sanctify them by Thy truth. Thy word is truth" (John 17:17). The link is further expressed in two modern maxims:

> This Book will keep you from sin,
>   or sin will keep you from this Book.

> There are two things that God cannot part;
>   Dust on the Bible and ice in the heart.

The linkage between being filled with the Spirit and with the Word is unmistakable. In Eph 5, Paul said that the filling of the Spirit is followed by "speaking to one another in psalms and hymns and spiritual songs, singing and making melody in your heart to the Lord" (v.19). In Col 3, he said that when the word of Christ dwells in us richly, it is followed by "teaching and admonishing one another in psalms and hymns and spiritual songs, singing with grace in your hearts to the Lord." Things equal to the same thing are equal to each other. Conclusion: To be filled with the Spirit is the same as letting the word of Christ dwell in us richly.

There is no holiness apart from the Bible. Said the godly McCheyne, "I believe God could sanctify without the Word. He made angels holy without it, and He made Adam holy without it; but He will not do it. 'Sanctify them through Thy truth, Thy word is truth.' Just like a mother nourishing a child, Jesus takes a soul and nourishes it with the milk of the Word." People are deluded if they trust an experience, then never open their Bible from one end of the week to another.

Pray Without Ceasing

Nor is there holiness apart from prayer. It was inevitable that when the Lord Jesus gave us a model prayer, He should include the petition: "And do not lead us into temptation, but deliver us from the evil one." No prayer is ever complete without a heart cry for preservation from sin.

Here are a few requests that we might add to our daily prayer list:

> "Lord, empower me to live a holy life."
> "Help me to remember that I am indwelt by the Holy Spirit and therefore I must do nothing to grieve Him."
> "Make me as holy as it is possible for a person to be on this side of heaven."

"Keep me from sin, even if I want to do it."

"Never allow the temptation to sin and the opportunity to sin to coincide."

"Don't let me die a wicked old man (or woman)."

"Keep me from doing anything that would bring dishonour on your Name."

"Take me home to heaven rather than let me fall into sin."

It is fair to say that no one can expect to live in holiness without wearing out his knees in prayer.

Stay Close to Christian Fellowship

Another sanctifying influence is the fellowship of other believers. Just as birds of a feather flock together, so should God's people. When Peter and John were released by the Sanhedrin, they immediately sought out their christian companions (Acts 4:23). We are exhorted not to forsake the assembling of ourselves together (Heb 10:25). In the book of Acts, whenever the Holy Spirit came down in a dramatic manner, it was when people were gathered together. It was what is known as "a communal experience of the Spirit."

The regular remembrance of the Lord's death in the Breaking of Bread reminds us what our sins cost the Saviour and is therefore a powerful deterrent to sin. The Lord's Supper is sometimes used of God to show us God's evaluation of sin and then through it we are strengthened to resist the evil one. But this is true of all the meetings of the local assembly.

Keep Busy for the Lord

Victorious Christians have proved the value of

keeping busy for the Lord (Eccl 9:10). Isaac Watts wrote:

> In works of labour, or of skill,
>   I would be busy too;
> For Satan finds some mischief still
>   For idle hands to do.

Which is another way of saying that one of the times of greatest temptation and danger is when we don't keep busy. David learned that lesson to his shame. In the spring of the year, when kings went forth to battle, David lounged, looked, and lusted (2 Sam 11). Before long, he had committed adultery, then tried to hide his sin by murder.

When we think of Sodom, we think of homosexuality, but Ezekiel reminds us that another of its cardinal sins was "abundance of idleness" (Ezek 16:49). No wonder it was a hotbed of immorality!

By keeping busy for the Lord, we can practice what is known as sublimation, that is, directing the energy of a physical drive from its primitive aim to one that is culturally and ethically higher. Especially those who are called to lives of celibacy must redirect their physical energies in untiring service! As someone has said, they must kill themselves with work, then pray themselves alive again. There is tremendous safety in days filled with productive work.

Practice Discipline of the Body

Link with that the discipline of the body. Said Paul, "I discipline my body and bring it into subjection, lest, when I have preached to others, I myself should be disqualified" (1 Cor 9:27). Today's English Version paraphrases it:

> That is why I run straight for the finish line; that is why I am like a boxer, who does not waste his punches. I harden my body with blows and bring it under complete control, to keep from being rejected myself after having called others to the contest.

Clearly Paul did not mean that he pommelled his body physically. Rather he was saying that he exercised self-control in such areas as sex, sleep, food, and exercise. He did not coddle and indulge the appetites of the flesh. For many of us this involves being willing to say "No" a thousand times a week. It involves rejecting the current wisdom of the world: "If it feels good, do it."

We must not forget that God rewards us every time we resist temptation. James said, "Blessed is the man who endures temptation ..." (1:12). And Ella Wheeler Wilcox wrote:

> Oh! when in the immortal ranks enlisted,
>   I sometimes wonder if we shall not find
> That, not by deeds, but by what we've resisted
>   Our places are assigned.

It means disciplining the time spent in sleep: an alarm clock can be a very spiritual piece of equipment. It means controlling the intake of food and beverages, remembering that "fullness of food" was another of Sodom's sins (Ezek 16:49). It means engaging in physical exercise, which the Apostle Paul admitted "profits a little" (1 Tim 4:8).

In short, it means this: When temptation knocks, send Jesus to the door.

Guard Your Thought Life

Equally important to the discipline of the body is control of the thought life. The fact is that we can control what we think, whether good or evil. The mind is the fountain from which our actions flow (Prov 4:23). James makes it clear (1:13-15) that sin begins in the mind. If indulged long enough it leads to the act. And the act, persisted in, leads to death. It is like the cycle of life: conception, birth, growth, death.

We become like what we think. As a man thinks in his heart, so is he (Prov 23:7). That is why it is important to exercise control over TV, video cassettes, radio, movies, magazines and anything else that stirs the animal in us. I sometimes humour young people by telling them that I find TV only twice in the Bible:

> "And the word of the Lord was precious in those days; there was no (tele)vision" (1 Sam 3:1b AV).
> "Turn away mine eyes from beholding Vanity" (Ps 119:37 AV)
> (TV – the first letters of the first and last words.)

When their TV tube went dead on New Year's Eve, a christian couple asked the Lord whether they should replace it or abandon the set. The very next morning their reading was in Ps 101. They received the requested guidance when they read vv 2b, 3a: "I will walk within my house with a perfect heart. I will set nothing wicked before my eyes."

In every life there are objects that have evil associations. Jude warns us that we must exercise mind-control by hating them (Jude 23).

But there is also the positive side in control of the thought life. We must not only expel evil thoughts; we must fill our minds with that which is pure and holy (Phil 4:8). This is "the scriptural power of positive thinking!"

Experience teaches us that we cannot think two thoughts at the same time. Make a practical application of that fact – we cannot think about sin and Christ simultaneously. Therefore, the more we think about the Lord, the cleaner our lives will be. We can go further by saying that the more we think about the Lord, the more we will become like Him. This is brought out by Paul in 2 Cor 3:18:

> "But we all, with unveiled face,
> beholding as in a mirror the glory of the Lord,
> are being transformed into the same image
> from glory to glory,
> just as by the Spirit of the Lord."

This verse is crucial enough in the area of christian holiness to deserve careful analysis.

But we all – that is, all true believers.

with unveiled face – sin causes a veil between our faces and the Lord. When we confess and forsake sin we have an unveiled face. There is nothing then between ourselves and the Saviour.

beholding as in a mirror – the word of God is the mirror.

the glory of the Lord – in the Bible, we gaze upon the moral excellence of the Lord Jesus, the perfection of His character, the beauty of all His works and ways.

are being transformed into the same image – as we gaze adoringly on Him, we actually become like Him. We are changed by beholding. As someone has said, "It is the look that saves; it is the gaze that sanctifies."

from glory to glory – this change takes place from one degree of glory to another. It does not take place all at once, but continues as long as we are occupied with Him.

just as by the Spirit of the Lord – the transformation of our character is effected by the Holy Spirit. He produces Christlikeness in all who gaze by faith on the Saviour as He is revealed in the Bible.

William D. Longstaff said it well in this verse:

> By looking to Jesus
>   Like Him thou shalt be;
> Thy friends in thy conduct
>   His likeness shall see.

Choose to Flee Rather Than Fall

There are times when the path of courage is to flee, to put a few healthy miles between yourself and oncoming temptation. Joseph did it (Gen 39:12). True, he lost his coat, but he gained a crown. He proved that "he who fights and runs away lives to fight another day." We are specifically told to flee fornication (1 Cor 6:18); idolatry (1 Cor 10:14); covetousness (1 Tim 6:11); and youthful lusts (2 Tim 2:22).

Jesus taught that we must often take strong, resolute action. He said, "If your hand or foot causes you to sin, cut it off and cast it from you. It is better for you to enter into life lame or maimed, rather than having two hands or two feet, to be cast into the everlasting fire. And if your eye causes you to sin, pluck it out and cast it from you. It is better for you to enter into life with one eye, rather than having two eyes, to be cast into hell fire" (Matt 18:8-9). He certainly didn't mean that we should literally mutilate our bodies; after all, they are temples of the Holy Spirit. But he was stating in a most emphatic manner that we must not trifle with sin but deal ruthlessly with it.

Someone suggested that when we flee from temptation, we should not leave a forwarding address.

Respond to Temptation as a Dead Person Would

But we still have not exhausted the list of things we must do as we press on. Paul reminds us that we should reckon ourselves to be dead to sin (Rom 6:11). The imagery is both vivid and unforgettable. Picture a corpse in a satin-lined coffin. A former mistress walks up to the casket and greets him. No response! She invites him out for the evening. The corpse lies silent and unmoving. She tries every device to incite him to sin. But it is all in vain; he is dead. This is reminiscent of Augustine's experience. One day he was accosted by a woman who had been his mistress before his conversion. When he turned and walked away quickly, she called after him, "Augustine, it's me, it's me!" Quickening his pace, he called back over his shoulder. "Yes, I know but it's no longer me."

We reckon ourselves to be dead to sin when we respond to evil solicitations exactly the way a corpse does. But we don't stop there. We reckon ourselves to be alive to God in Christ Jesus our Lord. That means that we respond to the Lord with instant obedience, seeking always to do the thing that pleases His heart.

Avoid the Touch of Danger

As another bit of practical advice, we should avoid petty familiarities – touches, caresses, endearing words, body language, kittenish behaviour. Writing in *Moody Monthly*, Jerry Jenkins lists a set of "rules" he follows as hedges to protect himself, his wife, his family, his employer, his church and the reputation of Christ.

1. Whenever I need to meet or dine or travel with an unrelated woman, I make it a threesome. Should an unavoidable last-minute complication make this impossible, my wife hears from me first.

2. I am careful about touching. While I might shake hands or squeeze an arm or shoulder in greeting, I embrace only dear friends or relatives, and only in front of others.

3. If I pay a compliment, it is on clothes or hairstyle, not on the person herself. Commenting on a pretty outfit is much different, in my opinion, than telling a woman that she herself looks pretty.

4. I avoid flirtation or suggestive conversations, even in jest.

5. I remind my wife often in writing and orally that I remember my wedding vows: "Keeping you only unto me for as long as we both shall live ..." Diana is not the jealous type, nor has she ever demanded such assurances from me; she does, however, appreciate my rules and my observance of them.

6. From the time I get home from work until the children go to bed, I do no writing or office work. This gives me lots of time with the family, and for my wife and me to continue to court and date.

Avoid Whatever Weakens the Will

In addition to avoiding any suggestive words or actions, we should avoid anything that lowers our innate resistance to sin, such as alcohol, mind-altering drugs, etc.

When under the influence of drugs or alcohol, people will do things that ordinarily they would not do.

Erin Lutzer comments:

> Noah's experience illustrates that drunkenness
> and immodesty usually go hand in hand. This is
> the first instance of drunkenness in the Bible and
> there you have it – Noah is lying naked in his tent.
> Alcoholism always lowers a person's moral
> defences. After a few drinks, inhibitions are gone
> and reasonable people are free to do what would
> be normally too embarrassing. Recently I
> overheard a man (of the world) discussing his
> immoral exploits: "We had some drinks and then
> we ..." Alcohol enables people to act like animals
> without feeling bad about it. Far from drowning
> their problems, alcoholics find that drink only
> irrigates them.

Call for Help

What should we do in the moment of fierce temptation when we are about to be overwhelmed and we
feel helpless? The answer is "Call on the Name of the
Lord." "The name of the Lord is a strong tower; the
righteous run to it and are safe" (Prov 18:10). When
Peter felt himself sinking beneath the waves, he
cried, "Lord, save me" (Matt 14:30). The Lord res-
cued him immediately. He always does.

Believe that God is Working In and Through You

Samuel Rutherford advised, "Expose yourself to
the circumstances of His choice." What does this
mean? Let John L. Baird explain: "It means that
when you and I present ourselves to God in the
morning, and present the day to Him, nothing can

come into that day that is not allowed by the permissive will of God. Everything has its place, and everything has its purpose. Such things may come in as cut right across our own little plans; such things as might disturb, as might change; but if we have committed our day to God, then we must believe that everything that comes into that day is allowed by His permissive will. We do not rebel against it, because that only embitters the soul, and loses the very blessing that God wants to give to us; but we expose ourselves to it ... Accept the circumstances, then, as they are."

Harold Wildish had a similar exhortation in the front of his Bible: "As you leave the whole burden of your sin and rest upon the finished work of Christ, so leave the whole burden of your life and service, and rest upon the present inworking of the Holy Spirit. Give yourself up morning by morning to be led by the Holy Spirit, and go forth praising and at rest, leaving Him to manage you and your day. Cultivate the habit all through the day of joyfully depending on and obeying Him, expecting Him to guide, enlighten, reprove, teach, use, and do in and with you what He wills. Count upon His working as a fact, altogether apart from sight or feeling."

To be filled with the Spirit is not excitement; it is holiness. Days may be filled with routine, mundane, even hard work. There will be occasional mountain peaks – enough to encourage us on. But the gears of life will mesh. Our service will sparkle with the supernatural. We will be conscious that God is working in and through us, but not in a way to create pride. When we touch other lives something will happen for God.

Also there will be power (Luke 24:49; Acts 1:8); boldness in witness (Acts 4:13, 29, 31); joy (Acts 13:52); praise (Luke 1:67-75; Eph 5:19, 20); and submission (Eph 5:21).

Now we shift gears to consider a different aspect of the subject of sanctification. The Christian finds himself in two kingdoms – the Lord's and the world's. It is essential for him to realise the difference and to know where his allegiance lies.

CHAPTER 12

Two Kingdoms

THIS IS the story of two kingdoms. One is called the world, and the other is the kingdom of God's Son. They are utterly different and irreconcilable. One is a sphere of moral and spiritual darkness, the other of light. A great gulf lies between them.

The World

When we speak of the world in this sense, we are not referring to Planet Earth, to nature with its beauty, or even to the world of lost mankind. Rather we are talking about the pagan civilization which man has built up in independence of God. It is human society with God left out. It is the whole sphere of affairs and activities by which man seeks to make himself happy without God. It has false principles, false values, and false gods. It is characterized by base desires, egotism and self-seeking. Actually it is man's ordering of things in opposition to God. Not only is the Lord neglected and forsaken; there is deep hostility against Him. It is more than alienation; it is war.

The Kingdom of Our Lord

When we speak of the kingdom of God's Son, we mean the society of people who acknowledge Jesus Christ as Lord and Saviour. For all practical purposes it is the Christian community. (Although there is a technical difference between the kingdom and the church, we will treat them as the same here.)

Satan and Christ

Satan is the ruler of the world, dictating its priorities and policies. He is called the ruler of this world (John 12:31; 14:30; 16:11), the god of this age (2 Cor 4:4), and the wicked one (1 John 5:19). He is a liar and a cheat (John 8:44) whose invariable aim is to steal, kill and destroy (John 10:10).

The Lord Jesus Christ is the Ruler of the other kingdom. His aim is to give life more abundantly (John 10:10). Although there are many so-called rulers, "for us there is only … one Lord Jesus Christ, through whom are all things, and through whom we live" (1 Cor 8:6b).

Who Belongs to Which?

All unconverted people are subjects of the world kingdom (1 John 5:19). They become members by natural birth. They are earth-dwellers in the sense that they are at home in the world. The psalmist spoke of them as "men of the world, who have their portion in this life" (Ps 17:14). They love the world and are loved by the world (John 15:19).

When a person is born again, he passes from the first kingdom to the second (John 3:3, 5), and pictures this transition by water baptism. Although he is still in the world, he is no longer a part of the system (John 14:18; 17:11). Rather he is a stranger and a pilgrim (1 Pet 2:11), journeying through the world to his heavenly home without taking any of the character of the world upon himself. He does not love the world, knowing that if he did, he would be an enemy of God (1 John 2:15). Instead he deliberately chooses to be hated by the world (John 15:18,

19; 17:14; 1 John 3:13). In a very real sense he is a non-conformist, refusing to allow the world around him to squeeze him into its own mould (Rom 12:2). He maintains an adversary relationship to the world, not co-existence or détente. He testifies against it that its works are evil (John 7:7) but also shares the gospel with it – how men can be delivered from the bondage of the world and find true freedom in Christ (2 Cor 5:18-21).

The world is very attractive, alluring, and seductive. For some Christians it holds a certain charm, and they feel disadvantaged to be completely cut off from it. So they seek to straddle the fence. They want the best of both worlds. For this reason the distinction between the world and the Church becomes blurred. That explains why someone said, "I looked for the Church and found it in the world; I looked for the world and found it in the Church." And Wordsworth said:

> The world is too much with us; late and soon,
> Getting and spending, we lay waste our powers.

If a child of God insists on fraternising with the world, God often allows him to do it so that he will learn by bitter experience that the world is empty. It is a façade. Its pleasures are shallow and brief. It cannot provide lasting satisfaction. It may be pleasing in prospect but it is bitter in retrospect.

> I tried the broken cisterns, Lord,
> But ah! the waters failed!
> E'en as I stooped to drink they fled,
> And mocked me as I wailed.

What's in the World?

The apostle John tells us that all that is in the world is the lust of the eyes, the lust of the flesh and the pride of life (1 John 2:16). Translation: the world glorifies sex, passion, violence, war, wealth, social status, and power. People of the world live for time, not eternity; for passing things, not for people; for self, not for God. All their plans end at the grave.

The Christian has a different sense of values. He is marked by love, not by lust; by purity, not passion; by concord, not conflict. He emphasises righteousness, peace, and joy in the Holy Spirit (Rom 14:17). Instead of the lust of the eyes, he is concerned with the desires of faith. Instead of the lust of the flesh, he is taken up with the desires of the Spirit. Instead of the pride of life, he seeks the glory of God.

What is Worldly?

In the past, there was a tendency to limit worldliness to such taboos as smoking, drinking, dancing, card playing, and movies. Now the pendulum has swung to the other side. These taboos are mocked by such jingles as, "I don't drink, don't smoke, don't chew, or go with girls who do." We are assured that these things are not worldly. What we should avoid are wrong attitudes, motives, and thought-patterns. This caused Erwin Lutzer to say, "Many Christians object to a given list of sins, not because they want to elevate christian conduct to the radical level of the NT but because they would like to lower their personal standards. Maybe they suspect that they are missing out on some pleasures, perhaps even sensual ones. So they criticise the taboos of the past for the wrong reasons. Their convictions continually shift on the quicksand of moral indifference."

Which World?

The world has different forms. There is the world of politics; by its very nature it is corrupt. There is the world of commerce; it is shot through with unethical practices. There is the religious world; its hands are stained with the blood of Jesus. There is the world of art, music and culture; the name of Christ is banned because it is an embarrassment. And there is the world of entertainment with its filth, sexual innuendos, double entendres. Hollywood and TV are portraits of this world in living colour.

How does the believer respond to the various aspects of the world? As to the political world, he remembers that neither Christ nor the apostles ever became involved. Did not the Lord say, "My kingdom is not of this world" (John 18:36)? And did not Paul remind us that our citizenship is in heaven (Phil 3:20). The solution to man's problems does not lie in politics but in the gospel of redeeming grace.

God's people cannot live in complete isolation from the business world, so Paul wisely counsels, "Use it but don't abuse it" (see 1 Cor 7:31). As soldiers on active duty we do not become *entangled* in it (2 Tim 2:4).

When we speak of the world of religion, we mean that sphere where the Christ the Bible is excluded. The Christian's standing order is to go forth to Him, outside the camp of organised religion, bearing His reproach (Heb 13:11-14).

As for the world of culture, art, and music, it is a question of what is of first importance. When Paul went to Athens, a centre of culture, he was not

stirred by its art forms, but saddened by its idolatry
– so saddened that he had to go out to Mars Hill and
preach the good news of salvation (Acts 17).

And what about the entertainment world? Entertaining people on the way to hell? Is this what life is
all about? Is Hollywood harmless? Does TV promote
purity? Is the theatre spiritually uplifting? The blunt
answer is that no one who feeds on this kind of filth
and garbage will ever make history for God.

A disciple must take his place outside the existing
order of things. Archimedes said that he could move
the world if he could get a fulcrum outside it. So it is
with the Christian. He can never move the world
unless he is separated from it.

Two Kinds of Wisdom

Next we come to the wisdom of the world as opposed to the wisdom of God. Perhaps the contrast
can be best seen by giving examples in columnar
form.

THE WISDOM OF THE WORLD	THE WISDOM OF GOD
Reality is found in what you see, touch and handle.	Spiritual values are what matter; everything else is temporal (2 Cor 4:18).
Wisdom is found in man's mind and intellect.	The fear of the Lord is the beginning of wisdom (Ps 111:10).
Greatness is to be master and lord, to be served.	Greatness is to take the lowly place, to serve (Luke 22:26, 27).
Truth is whatever seems to be culturally acceptable at any given time.	Truth is what God says about anything (John 17:17). It never changes.
The goal is large numbers, huge size. Big is beautiful.	The emphasis is on the minority, the remnant, the quality few (see Gideon's army, Judges 7:1-7).
Save your life by living for self, being true to self, and putting self first.	Lose your life for Christ's sake and the gospel's (Mark 8:35), esteeming others better than self (Phil 2:3b) and living for others.

Success is achieved by pushing for the top, for prominence, fame, status, and prestige.	Discipleship is a downward path of self-emptying (Phil 2:7).
Wealth is gained by accumulating possessions.	Soul prosperity is the true wealth. The believer lays up his treasures in heaven (Matt 6:20). He is rich, not in the abundance of material things but in spiritual treasures and in the fewness of his wants. In forsaking all, he gains all.
Seeing is believing. The man of the world walks by sight.	Believing is seeing. The child of God walks by faith, not by sight (2 Cor 5:7).
The end justifies the means.	Do only what is right, obey the word of God, and leave the consequences to Him (Acts 5:29).

Contrasting the world's wisdom with God's, Paul wrote: "... since, in the wisdom of God, the world through wisdom did not know God, it pleased God through the foolishness of the message preached to save them that believe ... we preach Christ crucified, to the Jews a stumbling block and to the Greeks foolishness, but to those who are called, both Jews and Greeks, Christ the power of God and the wisdom of God. Because the foolishness of God is wiser than men, and the weakness of God is stronger than men" (1 Cor 1:21, 23-25a).

The Methods of the Two Kingdoms

If the wisdoms of the two kingdoms are so diverse, it is inevitable that their methods and strategies will be also. Here are a few contrasts.

THE WORLD'S METHODS	CHRIST'S METHODS
Help those who help you.	Help those who cannot repay (Luke 14:12-14).
Retaliate. Give tit for tat.	Repay evil with good (Rom 12:20; 1 Thess 5:15).
Use violence if necessary.	Turn the other cheek (Luke 6:27, 29).

Distribute according to greed.	Distribute according to need (Matt 20:1-16).
Overcome obstacles through graft, bribery, and corruption.	Always do what is right (1 John 2:1), refusing to compromise or fudge.
Competition is the name of the game.	Cooperation and helpfulness without sacrificing any principles – that is the way to go (1 Cor 12:25).
Do as little as possible, at the same time trying to get the maximum return.	Work as for Christ (Col 3:22-24), seeking to maintain a good testimony in all things by diligence and excellence.
Judge by appearance.	Judge righteous judgment (John 7:24).

What Kind of Weapons?

The weapons of the world include not only guns and tanks but money, propaganda, publicity, the psychological manipulation of people, and dishonest practices. The believer's weapons are the word of God, prayer, faith, and love. These are "mighty in God for pulling down strongholds" (2 Cor 10:4).

Honours

Now let's think about the honours of the world. How does it inspire and motivate its subjects? It uses ribbons, plaques, diplomas, medals, trophies, uniforms, and titles. Napoleon once held up a short piece of coloured ribbon and said, "With ribbons like this I could build a kingdom!" Strange – when you remember that you can buy all the ribbon you want for a few pence in the local fabric store. Men and women are willing to run twenty-six miles for a laurel of leaves – a poor, withering wreath. Such are the world's honours.

Paul spoke of them as corruptible crowns, adding that Christians seek an incorruptible crown (1 Cor 9:25). God's word motivates believers to strive for the crown of righteousness, the crown of life, the crown of rejoicing and the crown of glory. Those who confess Christ before men will be confessed by Him before God the Father and all the holy angels (Matt 10:32; Luke 12:8). And what honour could ever compare with the Saviour's "Well done, good and faithful servant" (Matt 25:21, 23)? Faith enables the believer to say:

> O worldly pomp and glory,
>   Your charms are spread in vain!
> I've heard a sweeter story!
>   I've found a truer gain.
> Where Christ a place prepareth,
>   There is my blest abode;
> There shall I gaze on Jesus;
>   There shall I dwell with God
> *Hannah K. Burlingham*

The Ideal Citizen

The ideal citizen of the world is the wealthy, proud, and arrogant person who claims to be great. But not in Christ's kingdom! Here the ideal citizen is the poor in spirit, the mourner, the meek, the one who hungers for justice, the merciful, the pure in heart, the peacemaker, and the one who is persecuted for righteousness' sake (Matt 5:3-12). Jesus has special concern for the last, the least, the lowest, the poor, the downtrodden, and the disinherited (1 Cor 1:27-29; James 2:5).

Conclusion

Christ died to deliver us from this present evil world (Gal 1:4). We are crucified to the world, and the world is crucified to us (Gal 6:14). The cross is all our glory.

The world gave our Saviour nothing but a cross and a grave. God forbid that we should seek to be at home in such a system.

> We are but strangers here, we do not crave
> A home on earth which gave Thee but a grave:
> Thy cross has severed ties which bound us here,
> Thyself our treasure in a brighter sphere.
> *James G. Deck*

The world is under God's condemnation. The apostle John said, "The world is passing away, and the lust of it." And Donald Gray Barnhouse wisely added: "We are not to be interested in the world, for it is a condemned civilization, doomed to be destroyed by the Lord it crucified. The principles, ideals and methods of our life cannot be mixed with those of the world without being adulterated or contaminated."

"The world is passing away, and the lust of it, but he who does the will of God abides forever" (1 John 2:17).

It is essential that we live as citizens of heaven – as being in the world but not of it. But there is another subject we must not overlook, that is, the nature of sin and of true repentance. So, in a sense, we now pass from the Civics classroom to the one on Anatomy.

CHAPTER 13

The Anatomy of Sin and Repentance

WHAT IS sin? It is any act, word, thought, or motive that falls short of God's perfection (Rom 3:23). It is any violation of the will of God. It is not only doing what is wrong, but failing to do the good we know we should do (James 4:17). It is doing anything about which we have an honest doubt (Rom 14:23). It is lawlessness – the human will pitted against the will of God (1 John 3:4).

Sin is universal. "For there is not a just man on earth who does good and does not sin" (Eccl 7:20).

Sin is innate. Everyone is brought forth in iniquity and conceived in sin (Ps 51:5).

Sin is pervasive. Man is totally depraved. Sin has affected every part of his being (Rom 3:13-18). While he may not have committed every sin in the book, he is capable of doing so.

Sin begins in the mind (James 1:13-15). In his thought-life, man can wander down back alleys of evil where no human eye can follow. The more he thinks about a sin, and rolls it as a sweet morsel in his mouth, the more apt he is to commit it.

Sin is serious because it is against God (Ps 51:4a). Its seriousness is seen in the sufferings of humanity; the sufferings of the Lord for our sins; and the sufferings of the unsaved in hell.

Sin enslaves (Rom 6:15, 16a). It binds its captives

with chains of lust, greed, and all kinds of vile habits.

Sin is deceitful. It offers pleasure but provides no lasting satisfaction. It holds out the possibility of escape from punishment but fails to deliver. It may be lovely in anticipation but it is ugly in hindsight.

Sin blinds. We can detect it in others more easily than in ourselves. In us it appears quite respectable; in others it is repulsive. We excuse ourselves if we can only find someone who is worse. This comforts our depraved heart.

Sin hardens. When we first commit a sin, our conscience raises quite a fuss. The more we persist, the more muted is the voice of conscience. At length we can sin easily, and it no longer hurts. We have become past feeling.

Sin shifts the blame. When Adam fell, he blamed God and his wife: "... the woman whom you gave to be with me" (Gen 3:12). Eve blamed the devil: "The serpent deceived me and I ate" (Gen 3:13). Now their posterity blame the environment, their parents, or their fellow-men. For example, here are some explanations of car accidents submitted to insurance companies.

The pedestrian had no idea which way to turn, so I ran over him.

The guy was all over the road. I had to swerve a number of times before I hit him.

I pulled away from the side of the road, glanced at my mother-in-law, and headed over the embankment.

The telephone pole was approaching fast. I attempted to swerve out of its path when it struck my front end.

Sin never goes undetected (Heb 4:13). Secret sin on earth is open scandal in heaven.

Sin is never static. It works like leaven. A lie has to be covered up with other lies. When a person commits an immoral act he reasons that since he has gone that far, he may as well go all the way. Since people tend to condone their own sin, the more people who commit it, the less it is condemned, and the more accepted it becomes. Thus sin snowballs.

Sin brings suffering on the innocent, even to future generations. A drunkard's children share his misery. AIDS has been transferred to the innocent through blood transfusions. A drug addict shares damage with her unborn child. No one is an island. His actions, whether good or bad, touch others.

Sin has its consequences in this life and in the life to come. In this life it takes its toll on a person's spirit, soul, mind, and body. In the future it leads to eternal death and hell.

Apart from saving faith in the Lord Jesus Christ, sin's consequences are inescapable.

Now let us turn and see how sin worked itself out in the experience of David, king of Israel.

David had everything – good looks, wealth, fame, position, prestige, family and friends. He had risen from obscurity to the throne. Clearly he enjoyed the favour of God, and the future was filled with promise. The world was his oyster.

But he allowed himself to slip into a period of idleness and carelessness. At the time when kings ordinarily went to war, David stayed at home and luxuriated in comfort and ease. If he had kept busy, he would not have exposed himself to the peril that was lurking. But by failing to discipline his body, he gave the devil a beachhead.

Temptation! In an unguarded moment, while lounging on the palace roof, he looked across and saw a woman of extraordinary beauty. She was bathing.

His mind began racing! Fantasy after fantasy flashed before him. He wanted her. He must have her. Why shouldn't he have her? He was supposed to be happy, wasn't he? Isn't that what life is all about?

And yet red lights were flashing all over the place. His conscience was screaming, "No! No! No! You mustn't do it. It's sin. It's adultery. Stop." Even when he sent servants to bring the woman to him, one of them protested that she was the wife of one of his most loyal generals.

The ding-dong battle was on. There was no question as to what was right and wrong. The sane, reasonable, sensible thing to do was to draw back, to heed the voice of conscience. But there was the overpowering desire to have this woman. Even if it meant selling his birthright for the proverbial mess of pottage, he must have what he wanted. Nothing else seemed as important as one moment of passion. He was willing to sacrifice his happiness, his family, his reputation, for indulging his lust in a momentary gratification.

The Insane Plunge

So he took the insane plunge. Passion drowned out

the voice of purity. The lures of physical lust were more persuasive to him than the strong arguments of reason. Even the hope of heaven and the fear of hell seemed remote. For a moment of passion, he exchanged the honour of God, his own testimony, the esteem of his family, the respect of his friends, and the power of a sterling character.

Alexander Maclaren observes, "He forgets his longings after righteousness, flings away the joys of divine communion, darkens his soul, ends his prosperity, brings down upon his head for all his remaining years a cataract of calamities, and makes his name and his religion a target for the barbed sarcasms of each succeeding generation of scoffers. As man; as king; as soldier – he is found wanting."

Like Esau, he sold his birthright for a mess of pottage.

Sin had been beautiful in prospect; now it was hideous in retrospect. He felt dirty. Try as he would to rationalise, he was eaten by guilt. The consciousness of his sin left a bitter aftertaste. Perhaps he could arrange a perfect cover-up. He would send his loyal general into the thick of the battle where he would be sure to be killed. Then people would think that the unborn child was the general's own, and then David would be free to marry the widow.

The king thought that no one would know. But God knew, and God was angry. He loved David too much to let him get away with it. For about a year the Lord incessantly reminded him of his sins of adultery and murder, and David resisted like a roped steer. He was consumed by shame and disgrace, yet he refused to break, repent, or confess. Was it pride or sinful stubbornness or both?

Finally the Lord sent His prophet, Nathan, to him with a parable. It was about a wealthy man who robbed a poor man of his one and only lamb. Righteously indignant, David decreed death for the offender.

It was a trap, and the king had fallen into it. He was the guilty man. He could see sin in someone else but couldn't see the same sin in himself. In condemning the rich man, he had condemned himself. He stood speechless and defenseless.

True Repentance

At last he broke. The fountains of the great deep were broken up. He poured out his confession and repentance to God. It is preserved for us in Ps 51. Allow me to paraphrase it for you.

> Mercy, Lord! I ask for Your mercy! I deserve to be punished. But You are a God of steadfast love and on that basis I ask that You do not treat me in the way I deserve. Your mercy is super-abounding and because of that I dare to ask that you erase my awful violations of Your holy law.
>
> Wash me through and through from every instance where I have departed from Your straight line, and cleanse me from the frightful ways in which I have missed the mark.
>
> O my God, I publicly acknowledge that I have broken Your law. My sin was public and my repentance is public, too. The guilt of my sin has been haunting me day and night, and I cannot stand it any more.

I now see clearly that it was against You, and You alone that I sinned. Oh, I realize that I also sinned against Bathsheba and against her faithful husband, Uriah – God forgive me for my treachery to this valiant general. But I realize that all sin is first and foremost against You. Your law has been broken. Your will has been flouted. Your name has been dishonoured. So I take sides with You against myself. You are absolutely justified in any sentence You hand down, and no one can find fault with Your decisions.

Lord, I am no good. I was born in iniquity, and going back even farther, I was conceived in sin. In saying this I don't mean to cast any shame on my mother, or to extenuate my own guilt. What I mean is that not only have I committed sins but that I am sinful in my very nature.

But You hate sin and You love faithfulness in a man's inward being, so now I am coming to You to teach me wisdom deep in my heart.

You directed that hyssop and running water should be used in the ceremony for cleansing a leper (Lev 14:1-8). Well, Lord, I take the place of a moral leper. "Purge me with hyssop, and I shall be clean; wash me, and I shall be whiter than snow."

When I sinned, I lost my song. It has been so long since I have known what real joy and gladness are. Let me hear the music of rejoicing once again. In my backslidden condition, it seemed that You had crippled me by breaking my bones. I could no longer come before You in the holy festivals. Now heal those fractures so that I may join Your people in praising Your name in the dance.

O my God, I beg You to turn away Your face from looking on my sins in judgment and punishment. Blot out the last vestige of my enormous iniquities. How they stab me every time I think of them!

Looking back, I realize that the trouble all started in my mind. My thought-life was polluted. I entertained evil thoughts until at last I committed the sins. So now I ask that You create a clean mind in me. I know that if the fountain is clean, the stream flowing from it will be clean as well. Yes, Lord, renew my entire inner self so it will be steadfast in guarding against future outbreaks of sin.

Don't give up on me, Lord, or banish me from Your presence. I cannot stand the thought of being away from You, or of having Your Holy Spirit taken from me. In this age in which I live, You do take Your Holy Spirit from men when they walk in disobedience to You. You did it to Saul (1 Sam 16:14) – I shudder to think of the consequences. Please, Lord, spare me from this fate.

As I said before, I have lost my song. Not my soul, but my song. Not Your salvation, but the joy of Your salvation. Now that I have come to You in repentance, confession, and forsaking of sin, I pray that You will restore to me the joy of Your salvation, but also that You will uphold me with a willing spirit. In other words, I want You to make me willing to obey You and to please You in all things. Then I will be maintained in paths of righteousness.

One by-product of my forgiveness will be that I will aggressively witness to other transgressors and tell them the way of pardon and peace. When they hear of what You have done for me, they will want to return to You also.

Then, too, if You deliver me from bloodguiltiness, Lord, the whole world will hear my testimony of Your deliverance. The guilt of Uriah's blood is heavy upon me, O God of my salvation. Wipe the slate clean and I'll praise You forever.

My lips have been sealed shut by my sin. Open them by Your forgiveness and my mouth will be dedicated to speaking and singing Your praise.

Lord, I am not depending on rituals or ceremonies for forgiveness. I know that You are not a ritualist. If I thought You wanted animal sacrifices, I would bring them. But burnt offerings do not delight Your heart. It is true that You instituted sacrifices and offerings, but they never represented Your ultimate ideal. And so I come to you with a broken heart – that is the sacrifice You require. You will not despise this shattered and contrite heart that I bring to you.

And now, Lord, I want to pray for Your dear people as well as for myself. Be pleased to shower them with good things. Rebuild the walls of Jerusalem. My sins have doubtless hindered the progress of Your work. I have brought reproach upon Your name. Now may Your cause move forward without hindrance.

When we all walk in fellowship with You, confessing and forsaking our sins, then You will be pleased with our sacrifices of righteousness. Offerings that speak of complete dedication to Yourself will gladden Your heart. We will offer bullocks on Your altar – in praise to the God who forgives sin and pardons iniquity.[1]

This leads us quite naturally to consider the whole subject of sexual sins, including homosexuality. Since ours is a sex-obsessed society, it is imperative to face the subject head-on.

CHAPTER 14

The Area of Moral Purity

WHAT IS the battlefield on which Satan has won some of his most vaunted victories? Both the Bible and the history of the Church answer, "The area of sex". Sexual immorality has been one of his best weapons. Samson, David and Solomon stand out as examples of those who were tripped up by uncontrolled passion. Since then many christian leaders have failed to exercise self-control, have become involved in illicit relationships, and made shipwreck. The highway of holiness is littered with the corpses of those who have become castaways as far as service for God is concerned. That is one reason why it is important for us to have a biblical perspective on the subject.

God has placed within us certain drives or appetites, of which the sexual drive is only one. These drives are a gift of God and are therefore good, like all His gifts.

God's gifts can be used but they can also be abused. Fire and water are very useful when they are harnessed but they are devastating when they are uncontrolled.

The only proper use of sex is within the marriage relationship. That is one of the unalterable laws that God has woven into the fabric of human life. It is a kindly law, designed for man's spiritual, physical and mental well-being.

It was God who instituted marriage (Gen 2:18). He

did it before sin entered the world, a fact that gives the lie to any suggestion that the marriage act is something less than holy. "Marriage is honourable among all, and the bed undefiled' (Heb 13:4a).

In general, marriage is God's will for the human race. He intended marriage to be monogamous, that is, to one person at a time (Gen 2:24; Matt 19:5,6; Eph 5:22-33). He intended it to be permanent, that is, as long as both partners live. It was given for the good of all, not just believers. Although it is not exclusively a christian institution, the Lord Jesus hallowed and sanctified it at the wedding in Cana (John 2:1-11), and Paul taught that it pictures the relationship between Christ and the Church (Eph 5:22-33).

(True, some are called to a life of celibacy, but that is the exception rather than the rule.)

The Only Proper Use of Sex

Sex within the marriage relationship leads to pleasure and fulfilment; sex outside of marriage is a form of self-destruction. "Every sin that a man does is outside the body, but he who commits sexual immorality sins against his own body" (1 Cor 6:18b).

Sometimes we hear the suggestion that a marriage ceremony or contract is not necessary: if two people love each other, they can live together, and God recognises them as married. Marriages are made in heaven, they say.

But that is not what the Bible says. There was a definite ceremony and compact when Isaac married Rebekah (Gen 24:53-58). When asked, "Will you go with this man?" Rebekah answered "I will go." The ceremony included gifts of silver and gold jewelry and clothes.

God described His marriage to Israel as involving a covenant (Ezek 16:8b; see also Mal 2:14b).

There was a definite ceremony at the marriage in Cana of Galilee. Weddings involved feasts (Matt 22:1-14; Luke 14:8) that could last from seven to fourteen days. Guests were provided with robes (Matt 22:12). In Luke 12:36 we read of a master returning from the wedding.

Monogamy has always been God's will for people (Gen 2:24). It is true that polygamy and other marital disorders are recorded in the Scriptures. They are recorded but were never approved. God's will is that His people abstain from every form of evil (1 Thess 5:22).

Passing the Buck

Men still try to rationalise their disobedience. They twist the Scriptures to justify their free love, their living together without the ordinance of marriage. Chuck Swindoll gives a list of what he calls their "accommodating theology":

> * God wants me to be happy. I can't be happy married to her. So I'm leaving . . . and I know He'll understand.
> * There was a time when this might have been considered immoral. But not today. The Lord gave me this desire and wants me to enjoy it.
> * Look, nobody's perfect. So I got in deeper than I planned. Sure, it's a little shady, but what's grace all about, anyway?

       * Me? Ask His forgiveness? That's ridiculous. My relationship with God is much deeper than shallow techniques like that.

       * Hey, if it feels good, have it! We're not under law, you know.

       * So what if a little hanky-panky . . . a little fun 'n games goes on? What's life without some spice and risk? All those "thou shalt nots" are unrealistic.

To the list we could add the following:

       * It's OK as long as it's done in love.

       * We've been enlightened. We are no longer bound by the taboos of the Middle Ages.

       * Why can't I let my conscience decide?

       * Everyone's doing it. Why shouldn't I?

In spite of all these rationalisations, sexual immorality is still forbidden (1 Thess 4:3). It continues to take its toll. It is still true that we reap what we sow (Gal 6:7). It is still true that the way of the transgressor is hard (Prov 13:15b). It is still true that God will judge fornicators and adulterers (Heb 13:4b). It is still true that sexually-immoral persons will be excluded from heaven (1 Cor 6:9-10), and that they will have their part in the lake of fire (Rev 21:8).

In spite of their protestations, men cannot escape a sense of guilt and uncleanness. They cannot escape physical and psychological damage (Rom 1:27; 1 Cor 6:18). Venereal diseases still threaten them, in spite of medical advances.

But that need not be the end of the story. Just because a man has failed does not mean that God is through with him. If he is unsaved, he can repent of his sin and trust in Jesus Christ as his Lord and

Saviour. Then he can know that God has put that sin and all other sins behind His back. God has forgiven and forgotten. The case is closed.

If the man is saved, he can confess and forsake his sin, and have the complete assurance that he has been forgiven. God is faithful and just to forgive. He is faithful to His promise. And He can forgive righteously because the Saviour has paid the price and says, "Charge that to my account."

Divorce?

But what if the excitement has gone out of a marriage? Surely God would not expect a Christian to endure that important side of life joylessly and unhappily. Men reason like that and for any cause at all find in divorce an easy answer to their boredom. But men may reason as they will, God's word does not open up any escape route for the disenchanted. The Bible teaches clearly that God's will is monogamy and equally that marriage is until death parts. Every Christian must bow to God's will and not be lulled by the practices of society into thinking that divorce offers a way out if another man or woman seems much more appealing or the problems of the marriage are too great.

Sex Scandals

In recent years America has been rocked by scandals involving prominent church leaders. A well known TV evangelist has been exposed for an adulterous relationship eleven years ago. A writer on prophetic subjects left his wife for another woman. A prominent writer and lecturer on healing marital conflicts divorced her husband to marry another man. The head of a student organisation resigned because of an illicit liaison three years earlier. And so the melancholy list expands.

The general reaction among christian people is to draw a kindly veil over all such scandals. This is understandable. Some think that to say anything about them would be gossip. This too is understandable. But there is another side to the picture. By constantly hiding these moral failures, we may be doing the Church a disservice. If these horror stories were more widely known (without names being mentioned), they might serve as a warning to others facing similar temptations. Certainly the Bible uses the failures of others to deter us from similar episodes.

As we witness the fallout on the highway of holiness, we cannot but wonder, "Why do some fall and others don't?" Any who do survive unscathed are quick to acknowledge that their continuance is due to nothing but the grace of God. They keenly feel their own inability to resist temptation by their own strength.

Then it must be admitted that some are subject to greater temptations than others. Those who are in the front line of the spiritual warfare are special objects of Satanic attack. And those who are good-looking, gifted, and who have warm, affectionate, dynamic personalities may experience attacks unknown to others.

Some do not have the great blessing of having

other Christians praying for them.

But every Christian faces perils, even if some do more than others. Let us remind ourselves of these constantly.

Prayerlessness. It is always dangerous when we cease to acknowledge our constant need of the Lord's sustaining power. A healthy sense of our own proneness to sin and our need to cling to the Lord moment by moment is essential.

Neglect of the Word. A closed Bible shuts us off from warning, exhortation, and encouragement. Conversely, the Scriptures can speak loudly and appropriately to us when we are tempted to slip.

Isolation from the fellowship of the church. The sheep who is a loner is easy prey for the wolf. The blazing coal that is removed from the fire quickly cools off.

Uncontrolled thought life. Sin begins in the mind (James 1:14,15). Those who continue to feast on sexual fantasies almost inevitably convert the thought into action. That is why Jesus warned against the adulterous look (Matt 5:28). If a person never thinks adultery, he will never commit it.

Prolonged abstinence. In 1 Cor 7:5, Paul instructs married couples not to abstain from the marriage act except by mutual consent and in order to give themselves to fasting and prayer. Prolonged separation exposes them to Satanic temptation because of a lack of self-control.

Loneliness. Loneliness often leads a person to act irrationally and desperately. One cure for it is to immerse oneself in tireless service for the Lord and in self-forgetting service for others.

Undue familiarities. Jesus said, "If your hand makes you sin, cut it off" (Mark 9:43). A speaker at a seminary commencement advised, "Don't touch the woman. Don't touch the money. Don't touch the glory." The seemingly harmless caress, fondle, and pat can open the door to greater familiarity. A much-loved radio preacher couldn't keep his hands off the ladies. As a result, he was exiled to spiritual Siberia.

Failure to avoid compromising situations. Alone with the secretary in the office after hours. Alone with a counsellor with a growing mutual attraction. Alone with another man's wife in a plane, motel, or car. Situations that begin innocently enough can develop into full-scale conflagrations.

Margaret Hess advised:

> Draw boundaries in relationships with the opposite sex. A psychologist says he avoids scheduling a woman for his last appointment. A minister keeps a counselee on the other side of a desk and keeps the drapes open. A doctor calls a nurse into the room when he must examine a woman patient. A boss and secretary can avoid going to dinner as a twosome or working late evenings alone. A homemaker can avoid tempting situations with neighbours when her husband is out of town. A smart wife won't spend three months at a cottage, leaving her husband to fend for himself. Neither will she look after the husband of some other wife who has gone away for the summer. Nor need a husband show undue solicitude for a wife whose husband must be away on business. She needs to feel a gap that only her husband can fill.

Idleness. Allergy to work is a malignant ailment. Almost as serious is the inability to fill the day with constructive, fulfilling activity. We all need the discipline that keeps us busy enough to protect from temptation but not too busy to rob us of fellowship with God.

Pride. The adulation of other Christians can often lead a person to the dizzying heights of pride. He begins to think that he really is someone great, that the world is his oyster, and that he is fall-proof. His danger is enormous. "Pride goes before destruction, and a haughty spirit before a fall" (Prov 16:18).

Publicity. Anyone who lusts for publicity is "cruising for a bruising." Generally speaking, publicity is bad in christian life and service. Says C.A. Coates:

> The moment we want to put ourselves in evidence, we are wrong and out of accord with the present character of service. The Lord shrank from publicity; it is most touching, for it is so opposite to what we are naturally. We naturally like publicity, but the Lord on five or six occasions (in Mark) clearly enjoins on those healed that they should not speak of it . . . Publicity is a most damaging thing; it needs much grace if the Lord gives it, as He does to some.

Television. A continual diet of sex, passion, and promiscuity lowers the seriousness of sin in the viewer's mind and sets the lower nature on fire. Familiarity and constant occupation with the obscene leads to immoral behaviour. Sexy magazines, films, books, and video cassettes share equal shame with TV.

Entrapment. Christian workers know that they

have to be on guard against entrapment. A missionary in a country that is violently opposed to the gospel receives a phone call from a woman who claims to be in need of spiritual help. She is at the main post office. Would he please come and talk to her? He neglects to take his wife with him. When he meets the woman at the post office, the police immediately move in and arrest him for consorting with a prostitute. The government expels him. In this case there was no immorality but in other cases of entrapment there has been.

It is sad that a chapter like this has to be written. It would be far more comfortable if we could just pass over the subject as if no such problem existed. But the fact remains that a believer may fall into any sin against which he is warned in the NT, and immorality is certainly one of them. Nothing is gained by the attitude that if we don't look, the problem will go away. Better to face the fact head on and to guard ourselves against moral failure by living day by day in closest communion with the Saviour.

CHAPTER 15

God Spells Gay S-I-N

MANY PEOPLE claim that homosexuality is an acceptable alternative lifestyle. The so-called gays have come out of the closet and are clamouring for equal rights.

But believers must not be guided by what people say or what is currently being practised in our culture. They must not be swayed by the remark, "Everyone's doing it". The great test is "What does the Bible say?" So let us turn to the sacred Scriptures.

The principal passages dealing with homosexuality are:

Genesis 1 and 2. God created mankind male and female and established the marriage relationship as His will for His people. Thus homosexuality is a perversion of God's plan for sexual expression. It is a crime against nature.

Genesis 19:1-26. The men of Sodom were notorious for their homosexuality. Obviously the word "sodomy", meaning homosexuality, comes from the name of the city. When the men of Sodom tried to rape Lot's two male guests, God told His people to get out, then destroyed the city with fire and brimstone.

Leviticus 18:22; 20:13. Under the law of Moses, homosexuality was an abomination, punishable by death. (Incidentally, this gives the lie to the teaching that sodomy is a sickness. God does not condemn people to death for being ill.)

Romans 1:18-32. Primitive men had some knowledge of the true God, but they refused this knowledge and became idolaters, worshipping carved images of wood and stone. When they abandoned the knowledge of God, He abandoned them with the result that they began to practice all kinds of immorality, including homosexuality. Paul says quite bluntly that those who practise these things are worthy of death.

1 Corinthians 6:9. This verse says clearly that no homosexual or male prostitute will inherit the kingdom of God.

1 Timothy 1:10. Sodomy is listed with murder, adultery, kidnapping, and lying as transgressions of the law of God. The penalty for breaking God's law, of course, is death.

The Bible thus teaches quite clearly that homosexual behaviour is a sinful perversion of God's will for His creatures. No amount of rationalising can explain away the clear words of Scripture. Again we say that Christians must be careful not to accept the world's moral judgments but to be guided by God's word.

Can a homosexual be saved? The answer, of course, is yes, if he repents of his sin and receives Jesus Christ as his Lord and Saviour (John 1:12; Rom 10:13).

Can a Christian fall into this sin? It is conceivable that a believer could be overtaken in a moment of weakness. If so, he can find forgiveness through confessing and forsaking the sin (1 John 1:9). But if anyone lives as a practising homosexual, it is proof that he was never truly born again. Jesus said,

"Therefore by their fruits you will know them" (Matt 7:20).

Orientation versus Practice

Is there a difference between having homosexual tendencies and actually practising sodomy? Yes, it is an important difference. There are many people who have a homosexual tendency but who have never committed the act. They agonise over the fact that they are attracted to their own sex, yet they discipline themselves to resist the temptation and they live lives of purity.

Is the statement true, "Once a homosexual, always a homosexual"? If it means a practising homosexual, the statement is utterly false. Many gays have been converted to Christ and have completely abandoned their former lifestyle. The Holy Spirit has supplied them with the power to do this. Some of the Corinthians had been engulfed in sexual perversion before becoming Christians, and they had been delivered from it (1 Cor 6:9-11). As far as the homosexual tendency is concerned, a believer may have to battle with that the rest of his life, but he can find victory over it by redirecting his energies into untiring service for his King, the Lord Jesus.

How can God blame a homosexual when he was made that way? God didn't make anyone that way. When Adam came from the hand of God, he was innocent and undefiled. But then Adam sinned, and every one of his descendants, except Jesus, has been twisted, unrighteous and sinful. The blame lies squarely on man's own shoulders. To blame God for doing what He forbids is wrong, and an attempt to take away responsibility for one's own sinful actions.

Is homosexuality an inborn tendency or an acquired behaviour? Actually it could be either. It should not come as a surprise that a person can be born with this fault. Natural man is utterly depraved and is capable of just about any sin in the book. Some have a weakness in one area, others in another. No one is condemned for being born with a homosexual tendency, but he is condemned if he practises this sin. But homosexuality can also be an acquired behaviour. An adult, for instance, may lure a boy into this kind of life. Anyone who does this comes under the condemnation of Jesus when He said, "It would be better for him if a millstone were hung around his neck and he were thrown into the sea, than that he should offend one of these little ones" (Luke 17:2).

The Way of the Transgressor

Homosexual men and women pay a high price for their immoral lifestyle. Paul says that they receive "in themselves the penalty of their error which was due" (Rom 1:27b). This includes venereal diseases, pneumocystis (a form of pneumonia), Kaposi's sarcoma (a form of cancer) and AIDS (Acquired Immune Deficiency Syndrome). It also includes haunting guilt, mental and emotional disturbances, and abnormal personality changes.

After Oscar Wilde, English writer of the nineteenth century, had been exposed as a homosexual, he wrote:

> The gods have given me almost everything. But I let myself be lured into long spells of senseless and sensual ease . . . Tired of being on the heights I deliberately went to the depths in search for new sensation. What the paradox was to me in the sphere of thought, perversity became to me in the sphere of passion. I grew careless of the lives of others. I took pleasure when it pleased me and passed on. I forgot that every little action of the common day makes or unmakes character, and that therefore what one has done in the secret chamber, one has someday to cry aloud from the house-top. I ceased to be lord over myself. I was no longer the captain of my soul, and did not know it. I allowed pleasure to dominate me, I ended in horrible disgrace.

The way of deliverance from homosexuality is the same as that for any form of lust, and has already been discussed in the chapter on lust. However, on-going biblical counselling assistance is very important in every case.

What should be our attitude toward homosexuals? As Christians we should accept them as persons without approving their lifestyle. Because Christ died that they might be saved, we should seek in every possible way to win them to a life of holiness. We should deal with them in a spirit of meekness, considering ourselves, lest we fall into some form of temptation and sin. If they stoutly and steadfastly refuse the Word and become abusive and blasphemous, we are not obligated to press the gospel on them.

CHAPTER 16

Conscience, the Inner Umpire

CONSCIENCE IS the inner monitor that distinguishes between right and wrong in the areas of thoughts, intents, and acts (Rom 2:15). It causes a boy's eyes to scan the room as he dips his hand into the cookie jar. It causes the speeder to brake when what appears to be a police car appears in the rear view mirror. It causes the crook to flee when no one is pursuing. As Shakespeare said, it makes cowards of us all.

It is super-active at income tax time, or in a court of law, or at exam time in the classroom. No wonder the Bible calls it the lamp of the Lord, that searches out a man's inmost being (Prov 20:27).

Everyone is born with a conscience. Man knows intuitively that it's wrong to lie, to steal, to murder. Because he knows it's wrong for others to victimize him, he knows it's wrong for him to do it to others.

Not an Infallible Guide

But the conscience is not infallible. Like all our faculties, it has been damaged by the Fall. It can be affected by principles that we have been taught. So the old saying, "Let your conscience be your guide," is not adequate.

The conscience needs to be educated by the Word of God as illuminated by the Holy Spirit. "Conscience must be awakened and informed, brought into conformity with God's revelation, and followed" (Barnhouse).

True repentance involves the conscience. Reliving his experience, John Newton wrote:

> My conscience owned and felt the guilt
> And plunged me in despair.

Saul of Tarsus was goaded by his conscience and found himself kicking against the goads (Acts 9:5). When free grace awoke Robert Murray McCheyne with light from on high, then legal fears shook him; he trembled to die.

A purged conscience (Heb 9:14) is one that has been cleansed by the blood of Christ. Although it still monitors our behaviour, there is no fear of eternal judgment, since Christ bore that as the believer's Substitute.

> Conscience now no more condemns me
> For His own most precious blood
> Once for all has washed and cleansed me,
> Cleansed me in the eyes of God.

A weak conscience is one that is excessively scrupulous in matters that are not wrong in themselves (1 Cor 8:7, 8), matters such as food and drink.

A conscience can become desensitised through the owner's failure to listen to it. When I get in my car, a buzzer goes off, reminding me to fasten my seat belt. I got so used to it that after a while, I no longer heard it (that is, until a law was passed making seat belts mandatory!)

The more a man violates his conscience, the weaker its voice becomes. It is like a rubber band that gradually loses its elasticity. Or like flesh that has become seared or cauterised (1 Tim 4:2). The man can sin and be past feeling (Eph 4:19). He can commit an enormous sin, then wipe his mouth and say, "I have done no wickedness" (Prov 30:20).

It has been said that our greatest security against sin is being shocked by it.

A defiled conscience is one that is stained by evil deeds (Titus 1:15). If his life is evil, a man's conscience cannot be otherwise (Heb 10:22).

We should always have a good conscience (1 Pet 3:16), one that is void of offence toward God and man (Acts 24:16). A good conscience is in harmony with God's word.

CHAPTER 17

As a Man Thinks

THE CONTROL of the thought life is one of the most important disciplines that a Christian faces. The ways in which he uses his mind will inevitably determine the direction of his life and the bent of his character. Positive thinking that is according to Scripture (Phil 4:8) will produce positive results. An impure mind will inevitably lead to disordered behaviour.

It is for this reason that the Bible says, "As (he) thinks in his heart, so is he" (Prov 23:7). Or as Alfred P. Gibbs used to say, with characteristic punch, "You are not what you think you are. But what you think – you are!" The contents of a man's mind are an index to his character.

The wisest man said, "Keep your heart with all diligence, for out of it springs the issues of life" (Prov 4:23). Although the heart here does have wider application than the mind, still the verse makes very good sense if you substitute mind for heart: "Keep your mind with all vigilance; for from it flow the springs of life." The mind is the spring from which much of our behaviour flows. If you control the source, you can control the stream that flows from it.

The Tenth Commandment

It is not without significance that one of the Ten Commandments deals with the thought life.

> You shall not covet your neighbour's house; you
> shall not covet your neighbour's wife, nor his male
> servant, nor his female servant, nor his ox, nor his
> donkey, nor anything that is your neighbour's
> (Exod 20:17).

Coveting is an activity of the mind. It is the desire
to have something that is out of the will of God. God
says, "Do not covet."

This was the commandment that brought conviction to the heart of Saul of Tarsus. He had always
prided himself on living an outwardly respectable
life. He had never committed any of the grosser sins.
But when the meaning of the tenth commandment
dawned on him, he realised that evil thoughts are
sinful as well as wicked acts. As he pondered his
thought life, he was plunged into deep conviction of
sin.

> ... I would not have known sin except through the
> law. For I would not have known covetousness
> unless the law had said, "You shall not covet." But
> sin, taking opportunity by the commandment,
> produced in me all manner of evil desire. For
> apart from the law sin was dead. I was alive
> without the law, but when the commandment
> came, sin revived and I died. And the
> commandment, which was to bring life, I found to
> bring death. For sin, taking occasion by the
> commandment, deceived me, and by it killed me
> (Rom 7:7-11).

How It Works

James gives an incisive insight into the psychology of sin when he says:

> Let no one say when he is tempted, "I am tempted by God"; for God cannot be tempted by evil, nor does He Himself tempt anyone. But each one is tempted when he is drawn away by his own desires and enticed. Then, when desire has conceived, it gives birth to sin; and sin, when it is full-grown, brings forth death (James 1:13–15).

Here sin is compared to the cycle of human life. First there is conception. Then the baby is born. Then he grows to full maturity. Then he dies. It is like that with sin. It is first conceived in the human mind. Then the act is committed. Then the act becomes habitual. Finally it leads to death. It is implied, if not stated that if we think about a certain sin long enough, then sooner or later we'll do it. Or as the old saying goes:

> Sow a thought and reap an act
> Sow an act and reap a habit
> Sow a habit and reap a character
> Sow a character and reap a destiny.

In His teaching ministry, the Lord Jesus also put tremendous emphasis on the importance of the thought-life. One day He called a group of Jewish people to Him to get the point across. These people were punctilious about externals but quite indifferent about internals. Under the law of Moses they had always been taught that they would be defiled if they ate such foods as pork, rabbit, shrimp, crab meat, etc. And true enough, such foods did make a man ceremonially unclean during the dispensation of law. But now Jesus heralded the end of that dispensation by announcing that foods are no longer defiling but evil thoughts still are.

> And when He had called all the multitude to Him, He said to them, "Hear Me, everyone, and understand: There is nothing that enters a man from outside which can defile him; but the things which come out of him, those are the things that defile a man. If anyone has ears to hear, let him hear!" And when He had entered a house away from the crowd, His disciples asked Him concerning the parable. So He said to them, "Are you thus without understanding also? Do you not perceive that whatever enters a man from outside cannot defile him, because it does not enter his heart but his stomach, and is eliminated, thus purifying all foods?" And He said, "What comes out of a man, that defiles a man. For from within, out of the heart of men, proceed evil thoughts, adulteries, fornications, murders, thefts, covetousness, wickedness, deceit, licentiousness, an evil eye, blasphemy, pride, foolishness. All these things come from within and defile a man" (Mark 7:14-23).

You often hear people excusing sinful thoughts with pious explanations such as: "You can't stop birds from landing on your head, but you can stop them from building a nest there." This is meant to say that lustful temptations that come to the mind uninvited are not sinful; the sin is in welcoming them and responding to them. But the question arises, "If they are not sinful, are they pure and holy?" And the obvious answer is that any evil, lustful thought, whether invited or uninvited, is defiling, and needs to be judged and cleansed away by the blood of Christ. It is impossible to live in this world without being constantly defiled by suggestive advertisements, off-colour conversations, and other unwanted pollutions of the mind. But the remedy is immediate acknowledgement of the thought as unclean and instant rejection and expulsion of it as unwelcome.

Don't Even Think It

Jesus further emphasised the seriousness of evil thoughts in the Sermon on the Mount. He said:

> You have heard that it was said to those of old, "You shall not murder," and whoever murders shall be in danger of the judgment. But I say to you that whoever is angry with his brother without a cause shall be in danger of the judgment. And whoever says to his brother, "Raca!" shall be in danger of the council. But whoever says, "You fool!" shall be in danger of hell fire. You have heard that it was said to those of old, "You shall not commit adultery." But I say to you that whoever looks at a woman to lust for her has already committed adultery with her in his heart". (Matt 5:21, 22, 27, 28).

The law said, "Do not commit murder," but Jesus said, "Do not think murder." Why? Because if you don't think it, you'll never do it. The law said, "Do not commit adultery," but Jesus said, "Do not look on a woman with lust in your heart." Why did He say this? Because the act is first premeditated. If you slay the lust in your mind, you'll never have to repent of the act itself.

The apostle John echoes the same principles in his first epistle:

> Whoever hates his brother is a murderer, and you
> know that no murderer has eternal life abiding in
> him (1 John 3:15).

If it seems somewhat extreme to say that hatred is murder, we should remember that the two are linked together as desire and fulfilment, cause and effect. Hatred is murder in embryo form. Where there is no malice or passionate anger, there is no murder.

The human mind is indescribably mysterious and unspeakably marvellous. It is like the general headquarters of an army from which all orders are issued. The mind tells the hand to pick up the pen and to write. It determines what is being written. It is a vast communication system, sending a constant torrent of thoughts. And yet how does this all take place? And what is a thought?

It has been said that a computer designed to duplicate the functions of the human brain would have to be as big as the Empire State Building – and even then it would not be able to fully match the mind.

Most of us take our minds for granted. But the Bible clearly teaches that it is a faculty entrusted to us by God and for which He holds us responsible.

Each of us is like a king reigning over a vast and intricate kingdom – the kingdom of the mind. And each of us is responsible for what he thinks and for how he thinks. We can use it for good or evil, for worthy or unworthy ends. We can control what we think.

The Mind's Good Side

I think of the mind's potential for good. I think, for instance, of Handel sitting down and composing the oratorio *The Messiah*. The music is so wedded to the words that I can never read them in the Scripture without hearing the musical accompaniment in my mind. And the whole work is so superbly spiritual that I often wonder if we might even have this oratorio in heaven.

I think of Isaac Watt's great hymn *When I Survey the Wondrous Cross*. He dedicated his mind to the Lord and this song was only one of his contributions to the Christian world. But I say to myself, "It would be worth living a whole lifetime to write one hymn like this one."

I think of Milton's disciplined mind, the hours and hours of painstaking work, and then the finished masterpiece, *Paradise Lost*. How much the pages of literature have been enriched by his mind.

Or Michelangelo, his paintings and his statues. The range and beauty of his artistry beggar description. He had a mind for the universe, and fortunately for us, his thoughts have been crystallised in paint and marble.

And then I think of Charles Haddon Spurgeon, the

prince of preachers. I think of what A.T. Pierson said of him, "Of all the mind he had and all the chance God gave him, he made the most." And I can believe it when I read his sermons or study the account of his fruitful life.

Or to use an illustration from our own times, I think of the dedicated minds that planned and executed the various flights to the moon. What vision, what skill, what precision!

Potential for Evil

But then too we think of the mind's capabilities for evil. We think of heartless tyrants with their torture cells, their concentration camps, their gas chambers, their ovens. We think of the brutality that destroyed millions of innocent victims.

We think of men who devoted their talents to wrecking the faith of others – men like Voltaire, Tom Paine, and Robert Ingersoll. Gifted by God with keen minds, they prostituted those minds to the propagation of agnosticism and infidelity.

We think of men today who design, print, and publish pornography. What a way to use the mind! Peddlers of filth, polluters of the moral environment, promoters of impurity and perversion.

And then in general we think of the vast potential of any mind for evil thinking. No one of us would want to walk around for one hour in public with a sign showing the worst thought we have had during the week. We all know how the mind can take us down dark alleys of sin where no human eye can follow. It can conjure up all kinds of pleasurable situations, participating in forbidden relationships. Were a friend caught doing some of these things, we would condemn him with righteous indignation. But when we are alone, perhaps in the dark, we can mentally indulge in the same lewd and immoral behaviour and yet not feel the same revulsion. Unhindered by natural barriers of time and space, the mind can instantly transport us anywhere, to be with any person or persons of our own choosing, and to do anything the heart desires. It is frightening to think of the evil possibilities in the believer's thought-life. If these possibilities are habitually indulged, the result can only be disastrous. In 1988 a televangelist who preached to hundreds of millions worldwide was exposed in a sex scandal. He confessed that he had been fascinated by pornography since boyhood.

There are plenty of people today who are groaning under the bondage of some besetting sin. They say they want deliverance but they aren't willing to discipline their thought life. Recently a Christian took a seat on a plane next to a young soldier. After an exchange of greetings, the soldier handed a magazine to the Christian. As soon as he saw that it was filth, he returned it courteously, and offered the G.I. a small red Bible. A period of complete silence followed. Then the soldier asked the Christian, "Will you help me?" He poured out a lurid story of sin and shame, and pleaded for help. He wanted deliverance from sexual sin, but he still fed on pornographic magazines.

George Goodman reminds us that *thoughts can be controlled*: "Evil-thinking is like soaking rags in petrol; when the spark of temptation comes they are in blaze. You *can stop* thinking evil, and you ought to learn the art of thought-control, if you have not learned it already. There is no excuse for this secret indulgence of the mind in regard to the things of the flesh. By the Spirit every thought should be brought into captivity to the obedience of Christ. Every thought must be mortified by the Spirit."

Radical Action

Well, the crux of the matter is this: the axe must be laid to the root of the tree. There must be the willingness to deal decisively with the thought-life.

For the unsaved, it means first of all that he must be converted. Through faith in the Lord Jesus, he must be born again. Only then will he receive the power of the indwelling Holy Spirit to act resolutely against impure thoughts.

For the Christian, several steps are indicated:

First of all, take the whole matter to the Lord in prayer. The words of David form a fitting petition for every one of us: "Create in me a clean heart, O God, and renew a steadfast spirit within me" (Ps 51:10). These words form part of David's confession after his dual sins of adultery and murder. It seems to me that they contain an implicit admission that his sins began in an uncontrolled thought-life.

Second, judge every thought that comes into your mind as in the presence of Christ. The real test for thoughts as well as actions is how they appear in His presence. This is suggested in 2 Cor 10:5 RSV:

> We destroy arguments and every proud obstacle
> to the knowledge of God, and take every thought
> captive to obey Christ.

We should drag in every thought as a captive slave
to obey Christ's verdict.

Next we should confess as sin and defilement every
thought that does not meet His approval. Whether
walking down the street, riding in a car, wherever
we are, we should confess that stray, evil thought,
saying, "Lord, that is sin. My mind has been defiled.
Forgive me and cleanse me. I claim the power of the
blood of the Lamb."

And, of course, we must expel the thought from
our minds. The promise of mercy is not to those who
merely confess their sins but to those who confess
and forsake them.

He who covers his sins will not prosper. But whoever confesses and forsakes them will have mercy
(Prov 28:13).

Practically, this will mean learning to say NO ten
thousand times a week. Every time we are tempted
to think negatively, we must say, "No, I will not
entertain that thought. I reject it and cast it out in
the name of the Lord Jesus."

Positive Thinking

Then we must learn to think positively. Paul gives
us the word on this in Phil 4:8:

> Finally, brethren, whatever things are true,
> whatever things are noble, whatever things are
> just, whatever things are pure, whatever things

> are lovely, whatever things are of good report, if
> there is any virtue and if there is anything
> praiseworthy – meditate on these things.

The point is that you cannot think about these
things and think about sin at the same time. If
Christ and His purity fill the mind, sin and corruption have to go. Some call it "the expulsive power of
a new affection." Call it what you wish, but by all
means do it. The more we are occupied with Christ,
the more we are changed into His likeness (2 Cor
3:18).

Common sense tells us that if we want victory in
our thought life, we must exercise discipline over
what we read, what we see, and those with whom we
fraternise. Spicy books and magazines, Hollywood
films, the average TV show offer instant pollution.
And there are material objects that awaken lust in
people's lives. A good bonfire will help considerably.

Finally, we should keep busy for the Lord. The
times of greatest danger are moments of idleness
when the body is well fed and well rested. There is
tremendous protection and security in a life of tireless service for Christ. The man who has learned to
redeem the time has less struggle with random
thoughts that seek admission. Perhaps that is at
least suggested in Prov 16:3:

> Commit your works to the Lord, and your thoughts
> will be established.

This then is the way to keep your mind with all
diligence.

Search all my thoughts, the secret springs,
The motives that control;
The chambers where polluted things
Hold empire o'er the soul.

CHAPTER 18

Meditation, the Right Kind

I HAVE never known a holy person who did not spend time in scriptural meditation. There is a direct correlation between the time spent in contemplation and the godliness of the person.

When we speak of meditation, we mean the purposeful direction of the thoughts to edifying and God-exalting subjects. Christian meditation is a mental discipline by which the thoughts are focused on the Lord, the word of God, and the things of the Lord. Instead of allowing our minds to wander aimlessly down back alleys of trivia, we train them to reflect on profitable themes. Instead of idling in neutral, we shift our mental gears so as to progress in grace and knowledge. Meditation is the Christian's think-tank.

Picture a cow chewing its cud. It has already eaten food but now it brings it back from its first stomach to chew it again. Admire the contented look on the face of the cow. So the believer feeds on the word of God, then spends time ruminating on what he has read. This brings serenity and satisfaction to all of life.

The Wrong Kind

Of course, scriptural meditation is not to be confused with Transcendental Meditation or other forms espoused by Eastern religions. Cultic meditation often assumes that God is in the person and that through meditation he can realize his divine potential. Other forms tell the subject to clear his mind and wait for impressions. Telling people to empty their minds and wait for messages exposes them to the danger of demon invasion. Jesus told of a man who had been demon possessed, but who had experienced a sort of reformation. The unclean spirit was expelled, but the house was left empty. The unclean spirit returned with seven other demons worse than himself, and occupied the man's life (Matt 12:43-45). Christian meditation fills the mind with the word of God and with whatever is true, noble, just, pure, lovely, of good report, virtuous, and praiseworthy (Phil 4:8).

Meditation ensures spiritual prosperity and success. "This Book of the Law shall not depart from your mouth, but you shall meditate in it day and night, that you may observe to do according to all that is written in it. For then you will make your way prosperous, and then you will have good success" (Josh 1:8). Note here that one of the goals of meditation is to produce changed behaviour: "that you may observe to do according to all that is written in it."

Meditation deepens a man's roots in God. It makes him fruitful. "He shall be like a tree planted by the rivers of water, that brings forth its fruit in its season, whose leaf shall not wither, and whatever he does shall prosper" (Ps 1:3).

Meditation puts a person in the way to receive divine communications. God reveals His secrets to those who are near enough to hear (Ps 25:14a). They may be messages of guidance, encouragement, exhortation, or correction, but not of doctrinal truth.

He does not reveal truth beyond what is found in the Bible. The faith has been once for all delivered to the saints (Jude 3b).

Meditation saves a man from wasting time on trivial pursuits.

Meditation is a way of pleasing the Lord. Thus the psalmist prayed, "May my meditation be sweet to Him." And we should likewise pray, "Let the words of my mouth and the meditation of my heart be acceptable in Your sight, O Lord, my strength and redeemer" (Ps 19:14). And it produces likeness to Christ. The more we are occupied with Him, the more we become like Him (2 Cor 3:18).

How to Meditate

With regard to the method of meditation, there is probably no way that is best for everyone. Each believer must work out the approach that suits himself and his own circumstances. On the one hand we can set aside a definite period of time in a quiet place, free from telephone, television, radio, traffic, or other distractions. Isaac found a quiet place for meditation in a field in the evening (Gen 24:63). Or we can utilize free moments during the day or night. David used times of insomnia to remember the Lord and to meditate on Him (Ps 63:6).

It is good to keep a pad at hand to jot down uninvited reminders of work to be done, of calls to be made, or of any other thoughts that intrude. As soon as we write them down, we should dismiss them from our mind and get on with meditation.

There is no shortage of worthwhile themes on

which to meditate. The precious promises of God occupied the psalmist's mind during the night watches (Ps 119:148). The blessed man of Ps 1 delights in the law (word) of the Lord, and meditates in that law day and night (Pss 1:2; 119:78). The Puritans spent much time contemplating the attributes of God, and this accounts for the vast dimensions of their souls. The wonderful works of God in creation and providence afford inexhaustible food for thought (Ps 143:5). And the marvels of redemption offer infinite material for meditation. Paul told Timothy to meditate on the things that are vitally connected with dynamic christian ministry (1 Tim 4:15).

As a beginning it is helpful to take a short portion of Scripture, and using a little sanctified imagination, concentrate on each word, phrase or clause. For instance, "the Son of God . . . loved me and gave Himself for me" (Gal 2:20b).

the Son of God - Think of it! Not a mere man, but God manifest in the flesh. The Lord of life and glory. The Creator and Sustainer of the universe.

loved - Put together some adjectives that describe His love. It is immeasurable, unmerited, sacrificial, unparalleled, impartial. Review all that is said about it in 1 Cor 13:4-8a.

me - Ponder some of the ways the Bible describes us in our natural condition. Sinners, ungodly, dead, enemies of God, without God, without Christ, without hope, without strength.

and gave - Love always gives, but just think what His love gave – *Himself.* He didn't give money or any other material things. He gave Himself. That means

His blood, His life, His all. He paid the highest price to secure our redemption.

for me - Astounding! Only He would have given so much for one so unworthy. Now how should I respond to such love? I take the words of Isaac Watts as my own:

> Were the whole realm of nature mine,
> That were an off'ring far too small.
> Love so amazing, so divine
> Demands my soul, my life, my all.

If this method seems difficult for a new believer with limited Bible knowledge, then he can take some Scripture narrative, try to visualise it, and draw lessons from it as he goes along. For example, he could read the call of Matthew (Levi) in Luke 5:27, 28. Picture his collecting taxes or customs. He meets many people. Then Jesus comes along. What does Matthew detect about Him that is different? All Jesus says is "Follow Me." What must have gone through Matthew's mind? What would have gone through my mind? What did he give up by following Jesus? What did he gain?

This method of visualisation is not to be confused with that which is connected with possibility thinking. The gurus of this latter technique teach that visualising what we want will actually produce it, whether health, prosperity, fame, prestige, or pleasure. This, of course, has no Scriptural basis whatever.

Dr W.E. Sangster writes,

> The devout student has learned to live in the

Bible. By a reverent use of the imagination, he has developed a method of slipping within the covers of the Book and making it autobiographical. The noblest use of the imagination is not to plan things for the future but to run back through the corridors of time and call up the scenes and facts of our Lord's life, and to be present as if in body at every recorded event of the history of our Redeemer; to run back through time and jostle with Peter and James and John when they stand around the Saviour; to see Lazarus emerging from the tomb; to sit with Mary at Jesus' feet. The proper use of the imagination is to take true things and make them vivid in the life of today. We can read the Bible from the outside or the inside. We can come to it in a detached fashion and always be external to it, or we can slip between its covers and live within the divine Word itself.[2]

The Barrenness of a Busy Life

One of the greatest hindrances to meditation is our excessive busyness. We experience the barrenness of a busy life. Our careers consume us. The demands of home and family press in on us – buying a home, maintaining a car or two, providing food, clothing, insurance, education, etc. Even in so-called full-time christian work it is easy to fall under what Charles Hummel called the tyranny of the urgent. The preparation of messages, the ministry of discipling, the demands of counselling, the thousand and one calls for assistance leave little time for sitting at the Saviour's feet.

We become workaholics. We are like the Japanese cars that boasted the slogan, "We're driven." We allow the mundane details of housekeeping and shopping to crowd out the things that really matter. But we must not excuse ourselves just because we're driven. Busy people can still meditate. It's largely a matter of time management. Even Type A persons (highly motivated achievers) have spare time and in-between moments. We must learn to discipline ourselves to redeem these times for the heavenward gaze. If we're too busy to do this, then we're really too busy.

> God does not reveal Himself hurriedly to the man on the jump. He does not unveil His heart to the one who wants only a curious, casual glance. He does not manifest His glory to the spiritual tourist, but to the one who comes up to Him on the Mount. The reflected glory on Moses' face as he came forth from his forty days of communion with God was not produced by a snapshot, but by a time exposure (see P. 158).

Direct Line from Heaven

We mentioned previously that meditation often puts people in a position to receive special communications from the Lord. Here we must be careful because we sometimes hear shallow, even carnal Christians say, "The Lord told me . . ." But both the Bible and subsequent experience prove that the Lord didn't tell them anything of the kind. However, that doesn't deny the fact that those who enjoy special intimacy with God do receive revelations from Him. Let me close with three examples.

Mrs Shepherd believed that the Lord had given her assurance that her large family of children would be saved. However, when she shared this with a preacher, he pooh-poohed the idea. Her ailing brother, who lived across town knew nothing of this. But one night as he was meditating on Isa 49, he asked his wife to take a message to his sister. The message was v.25: "I will contend with him who contends with you, and I will save your children." All her children were saved in subsequent years.

Alfred enjoyed unusual nearness to the Lord. His closest friend, Alex, who also dwelt in the secret place of the Most High, lived thousands of miles away. One day the aged Alfred said to his daughter, "You know, I haven't met Alex at the throne of grace for three months." Shortly thereafter a letter confirmed that Alex had died three months previously.

It was a Saturday afternoon. A young believer was in his downtown office, wrestling with God in great agony of soul. He felt that the Lord had forsaken him. The phone rang. It was Allan Smith, an older man who practically lived in the book of Psalms. He said, "I just want you to know that the Lord has laid you on my heart, and I am praying for you." The young man was astonished. Allan was only a casual acquaintance. There was no way, humanly speaking, that he could know of the young brother's trauma. And there was no reason to believe that he could reach him in the office on a Saturday afternoon.

Said Murdo MacLeod:

> Those who walk with the Lord by faith, and who know Him as their Companion in the way, cannot fail to enjoy intimations of His love and care. To such He is not silent. To such He is not a stranger . . . In christian experience of any depth, there is often an element of mystery unknown to the world, or to those who have only a name to live.

CHAPTER 19

The Taming of the Tongue

NO ONE will be surprised to learn that a Christian's speech is a barometer of his character, because "out of the abundance of the heart, the mouth speaks" (Matt 12:34b). By simply listening to a person's talk, you can tell where he is spiritually.

James reminds us of what we have already learned by experience – that though the tongue is small, it is capable of great good and great evil. Although man can tame all creatures in wildlife, no man can tame the tongue. "It is an unruly evil, full of deadly poison." Unlike other things in nature, the tongue can produce opposites, such as sweet and bitter, blessing and cursing (James 3:1-12).

Even if we can't tame the tongue, we can be everlastingly grateful that God can. By the power of the Spirit, He can make the sharp tongue gracious and the gossiping tongue edifying.

Here are some of the qualities that should characterise our speech:

It Should Be Truthful

"Therefore, putting away lying, each one speak truth with his neighbour, for we are members of one another" (Eph 4:25). God cannot lie and He cannot grant that permission to anyone else. This rules out fibs, white lies, exaggerations, flattery, and broken promises. Reports of results in christian service must not be overdrawn. The secretary must not say the boss is not in when he is. And children must not be prompted to lie to an unwelcome visitor.

If a person is honest he doesn't have to have a good memory. Said E. Stanley Jones, "If you tell lies you have to have a good memory to cover up the lies; but if you tell the truth every time, you do not have to have a good memory – you just tell the truth. That is simple."

It Should Be Worthwhile

"Let no corrupt communication proceed out of your mouth . . ." (Eph 4:29a). Here the word *corrupt* means of poor quality, unfit for use, worthless. When tape recorders first came out, it was a fun game to hide one and record the conversation at the table. When the tape was replayed, the speakers were often embarrassed by the sheer emptiness of their talk. Jesus warned that "for every idle word men may speak, they will give account of it in the day of judgment" (Matt 12:36). Therefore, empty chatter should be confessed as sin and put away from our lives.

It Should Be Edifying

. . . "but what is good for necessary edification" (Eph 4:29b). In other words, we should constantly seek to build up others by what we say. H. A. Ironside always directed a conversation to edifying subjects. He would often ask, "What do you think this verse means?" and then quote a problem text. If the other person didn't know, he would graciously suggest, "Do you think it might mean this?" His explanations were unforgettable.

A friend of mine started to say something negative about another person. It sounded as if it was going to be a juicy bit of gossip. But he stopped in the middle of the sentence and said, "No! That wouldn't be edifying." I've been dying of curiosity ever since, but I learned a valuable lesson that day on how to discipline the tongue.

It Should Be Appropriate

"Let no unwholesome word proceed from your mouth, but only such a word as is good for edification *according to the need of the moment . . .*" (Eph 4:29c NASB). It is a great gift to be able to say the right thing at the right moment. Like the godly elder who leaned over the bed of a dying saint and quoted Song of Solomon 8:5, "Who is this coming up from the wilderness, leaning upon her beloved?" Or the beloved pastor who broke the grief of a bereaved family with Ps 30:5, "Weeping may endure for a night but joy comes in the morning." Or the christian woman who wrote Isaiah 49:4 at the end of a letter to a discouraged preacher, "Then I said, 'I have laboured in vain, I have spent my strength for nothing and in vain; yet surely my just reward is with the Lord, and my work with my God.'" When Dr. Alexander Whyte walked into a lawyer's office, he was staggered by the question, "Have you any message for an old sinner?" He repeated the text on which he had been meditating, "He delights in mercy" (Micah 7:18). The lawyer thanked him for the only word that would have given him comfort. These words were according to the need of the moment. So "a word fitly spoken is like apples of gold in settings of silver" (Prov 25:11). And "a word spoken in due season, how good it is" (Prov 15:23).

It Should Be Gracious

Not only should our speech be appropriate; it should be *gracious*. "Let your speech always be with grace . . . " (Col 4:6a). Our Lord was gracious, so much so that men "marvelled at the gracious words which proceeded out of His mouth" (Luke 4:22b). Was it not grace for Him, a Jew, to ask for a drink of water from a despised Samaritan woman (John 4:7)? And what was it but grace when He said to the cowering woman caught in adultery, "Neither do I condemn you" (John 8:11b)? Graciousness requires that we refrain from sharp, cutting remarks; from unkind innuendos; from barbed sarcasm. Said Lady Astor, "Sir Winston, if I were your wife, I'd put poison in your coffee." To which Mr Churchill replied "Lady Astor, if I were your husband, I'd drink it." Terribly funny but not terribly gracious!

Our speech should be gracious, yes, but also *seasoned with salt*. "Let your speech always be with grace, seasoned with salt" (Col 4:6b). The same Lord who said, "Give me a drink" also said "Go, call your husband" (John 4:16). And after saying, "Neither do I condemn you" He added "Go and sin no more." The words have a certain sharpness to them. They are spicy.

Of course, salt is also a preservative; it hinders corruption. And salt creates thirst. So by our speech we should preserve standards of moral integrity, and stimulate a thirst for the living waters which Christ offers.

It Should Be Pure

Of course, the believer's speech should be *pure*. "But fornication and all uncleanness or covetousness, let it not even be named among you, as is fitting for saints; neither filthiness, nor foolish talking, nor coarse jesting, which are not fitting, but rather giving of thanks" (Eph 5:3, 4). The more freely we talk about sin and immorality the less serious they seem to us and to those who hear us. They acquire a deadly familiarity, and we cease to be horrified by them. It is true that the Bible sometimes discusses heinous sins, but always in a way to create loathing of them, never in such a way as to condone or make light of them.

It Should Not Use Oaths

Our conversation should be *unconfirmed by oaths* ". . . do not swear at all: neither by heaven . . . nor by earth . . . nor shall you swear by your head . . . But let your 'Yes' be 'Yes', and your 'No', 'No'. For whatever is more than these is from the evil one" (Matt 5:34-37). "But above all, my brethren, do not swear, either by heaven or by earth or with any other oath. But let your 'Yes' be 'Yes', and your 'No', 'No', lest you fall into judgement" (James 5:12). A Christian's speech should be consistently honest that he never needs to confirm it with an oath. As someone has said, "Oaths are of no use. A good man does not need one and a bad man would not heed one."

We all know that it is wrong to take the name of the Lord in vain and to use offensive four-letter words. But what about minced oaths, that is, euphemisms for forbidden words? For example, gosh and golly for God; gee, geez for Jesus; jeepers creepers for Jesus Christ; darn for damn; heck for hell. These violate the Scriptures just as surely as their more obvious counterparts.

Well, what about taking an oath in a court of law? When our Lord was on trial, the high priest said "I adjure you by the Living God that you tell us if you are the Christ, the Son of God." To adjure means to command under oath. As a Jew under the Law, Jesus was required to testify under oath (Lev 5:1), and He did so. This settles the matter for many Christians. But if they still have a conscience against taking a legal oath, they are allowed to testify by affirmation. This means answering questions or giving evidence without swearing to God.

It Should Be Reverent

We should not talk lightly or disrespectfully about sacred things. We should not make puns on Scripture, that is, quote Bible verses in a humorous, out-of-context manner. We should be serious about divine matters.

No one is opposed to some clean humour, but the truth is that excessive levity leads to a leakage of spiritual power. The Holy Spirit has often been quenched in meetings through a barrage of funny stories. The solemnity of a gospel appeal has been dispelled by entertaining anecdotes.

Servants of Christ should avoid making quips and smart aleck remarks. The lust to intrude into every conversation with wisecracks, or to go one better in telling jokes earns for one the deserved reputation of a spiritual featherweight.

It Should Be Brief and to the Point

"In the multitude of words, sin is not lacking, but he who restrains his lips is wise" (Prov 10:19). In other words, the more we talk, the more apt we are to sin. We can avoid this danger by resisting the urge to be always saying something. "Do not be rash with your mouth, and let not your heart utter anything hastily before God. For God is in heaven and you on earth; therefore let your words be few" (Eccl 5:2). While this refers especially to vows made to God, the advice is good for general use.

Actually a compulsive talker is a bore. He never comes up for air. No one else has a chance to get a word in edgeways. He monopolises every conversation and every unfortunate listener's time and attention.

In conclusion, let me quote a pithy summary. I don't know who wrote it, but I wish I had been the one.

> What should a Christian do with his tongue? He should control it, never seeking to dominate in conversation. He should train it to say less than it might. He should never use it for falsehood, half-truth, malice, innuendos, sarcasm, unclean talk, or empty chatter. He should always use it where

circumstances call for testimony, confession, or the word of encouragement. If he is one of those strange people who find it difficult to say 'thank you', he should train the tongue to utter the words, and deal with the vicious pride which inhibits them.

The tongue should follow thought, not lead it. More have repented speech than silence. He who speaks sows, but he who listens reaps.

CHAPTER 20

Forgive Us Our Gossip!

SOME YEARS ago the following appeared in the *Atlanta Journal:*

> I am more deadly than the screaming shell of a howitzer. I win without killing. I tear down homes, break hearts, and wreck lives. I travel on the wings of the wind. No innocence is strong enough to intimidate me, no purity pure enough to daunt me. I have no regard for truth, no respect for justice, no mercy for the defenceless. My victims are as numerous as the sands of the sea, and often as innocent. I never forget and seldom forgive. My name is Gossip!

Perhaps James was thinking particularly of the sin of gossip when he wrote, "... we all stumble in many things. If anyone does not stumble in word, he is a perfect man, able also to bridle the whole body" (James 3:2).

It is so easy and natural to gossip, so difficult to kick the habit.

What is gossip? William R. Marshall says that it is the art of saying nothing in a way that leaves nothing unsaid. Bill Gothard says it is sharing information with someone who is neither part of the problem nor of its solution. We can expand the definition to say that it is talking in a derogatory manner *about someone who is absent.* Gossip puts its victim in an unfavourable light; it says things that are not kind,

edifying, or necessary. It is criticising a person behind his back rather than confronting him face to
face. It is a form of character assassination.

The Bible comes down hard on the practice.

> "You shall not go about as a talebearer among
> your people" (Lev 19:16a).

> A talebearer reveals secrets,
> But he who is of a faithful spirit
>   conceals a matter (Prov 11:13. See also 20:19).

> A perverse man sows strife,
> And a whisperer separates
>   the best of friends (Prov 16:28).

> The words of a talebearer
>   are like tasty trifles,
> And they go down into the
>   inmost body (Prov 18:8).

> Where there is no wood,
>   the fire goes out;
> And where there is no
>   talebearer, strife ceases (Prov 26:20).

In Rom 1:29 Paul lists gossips (whisperers) along
with murderers and immoral persons.

Don't Tell Anyone I Told You

Sometimes we try to camouflage gossip by
pretending that we are sharing information as
a matter for prayer. "I mention this only so
that you can pray about it, but did you know
that ..." Or we think we are avoiding offense by

telling it in confidence. The following is often the result.

> Two women were talking in Brooklyn:
> "Tillie told me you told her that secret I told you not to tell her."
> "She's a mean thing. I told Tillie not to tell you I told her."
> "Well, I told Tillie I wouldn't tell you she told me — so don't tell her I did."

In his book, *Seasons of Life,* Charles Swindoll deals with rumour-mongers but that is just another name for gossips. Here is what he says:

> Those who feed on rumours are small, suspicious souls. They find satisfaction in trafficking in poorly-lit alleys, dropping subtle bombs that explode in others' minds by lighting the fuse of suggestion. They find comfort in being only an "innocent" channel of the unsure information ... *never* the source. The ubiquitous "They say" or "Have you heard?" or "I understand from others" provides safety for the rumour-spreader.

> "Have you heard that the Hysterical Concrete Memorial Church is about to split?"

> "I understand that Ferdinand and Flo are divorcing ... they say she was unfaithful."

> "They say his parents have a lot of money."

> "Did you hear that Pastor Elphinstonsky was asked to leave his former church?"

"I was told their son is taking dope ... got picked up for shoplifting."

"Someone said they *had* to get married."

"Somebody mentioned he is a heavy drinker."

"I heard she's a flirt ... watch out for her."

"The word is out ... he finally cheated his way to the top."

"It's a concern to several people that he can't be trusted."

We all know how gossip and rumours grow as they travel from one to another. Each person adds a negative touch until the final story has little resemblance to the original.

Paul Mentioned Names – But Why?

Someone may object that Paul spoke critically about Hymenaeus and Alexander (1 Tim 1:19, 20); about Phygellus and Hermogenes (2 Tim 1:15); and Alexander the coppersmith (2 Tim 4:14). And John did not spare Diotrephes (3 John 9, 10). This testimony is true. But the purpose was to warn believers about these men, not to scurrilously attack them.

It is often necessary for leaders to discuss individuals when discipline or correction are necessary. But this is intended to help the persons involved, not to tear them down. This is not the same as gossip.

There are certain positive steps we can take in dealing with gossips.

First, we can ask the person to identify the source. Paul set an example for us in 1 Cor 1:11: "For it has been declared to me concerning you, my brethren, by those of Chloe's household, that there are contentions among you."

Second, we can ask permission to quote the gossiper to the person being discussed. "Would you mind if I were to tell him what you just said about him?" "Oh, horrors, don't do that. That would be the end of our friendship!"

Or we can refuse to listen to gossip. We can do this by saying courteously that we'd rather not hear it, or we can redirect the conversation into more edifying channels. "If nobody ever listened to gossip, nobody would ever tell it. Make the audience deaf, and you make the gossiper dumb" (William R. Marshall).

A Turkish proverb reminds us, "Who gossips *to* you will gossip *of* you."

CHAPTER 21

The Temper - ature Test

IT WAS in a church meeting, and he was not having his own way. He was livid with rage. His arms flailed erratically as he poured out a torrent of abuse. His eyes glared, his jowls shook, and his knuckles whitened. Finally, he stomped out, shouting, "I go and the Lord goes with me." But no one considered him a holy man. And no one believed that the Lord would care to accompany anyone who was in such a temper tantrum.

The scene shifts. It is Sunday morning. The family is getting ready for church. The kids are dawdling, father is shouting, mother is having trouble with the oven, and the house is in an uproar. But not to worry. Soon they are all lined up in their pew with cherubic smiles, haloes all in place.

Now it is Christmas time. Everyone has been frantically shopping for unneeded gifts, buying something for people who have everything. Pressure mounts. Nerve ends are raw. Tempers are short. One unkind remark, and the boiler blows. The fight is on! And thus they celebrate the birth of the meek and lowly Jesus!

Life is filled with TEMPER-ature tests, cleverly disguised as frustrations. Someone has just scratched your new car in the parking lot. Your plane is late. The waiter is extraordinarily clumsy, spilling soup on your lap. Your phone rings at 3.30 a.m.: "Sorry. I must have the wrong number." You no sooner hang up when it rings again. Same nitwit. Junior has spilled paint on a prized possession and the dog has chewed up the work of years.

Nothing is a poorer advertisement for the Christian faith than a display of temper. And nothing speaks louder for the transforming power of Christ than a person who reacts with calm and poise under trying circumstances. No wonder the Scriptures say, "He who is slow to anger is better than the mighty and he who rules his spirit than he who takes a city" (Prov 16:32).

A Time for Anger

Someone may object that we are commanded to be angry in Eph 4:26: "Be angry, and do not sin; do not let the sun go down on your wrath." That is true. There is a time to be angry. We should be angry when the Lord is being dishonoured. Thus Jesus was angry when man made His Father's house a den of thieves (Matt 21:13). And we should be angry when other people are being mistreated. In short, we are entitled to be angry on behalf of the Lord and of others, but never for ourselves. We should be lions in God's cause, and lambs in our own. And even then there is the danger of righteous anger spilling over into sinful wrath. Wrath is anger with the lid off. That is why Paul says, "Be angry, *and do not sin; do not let the sun go down on your wrath.*"

Against the one command to be angry, there are a host of verses instructing us to be longsuffering and slow to anger.

"Let all bitterness, wrath, anger, clamour, and evil speaking be put away from you, with all malice. And be kind to one another, tenderhearted, forgiving one another, even as God in Christ forgave you" (Eph 4:31, 32).

"The fruit of the Spirit is . . . longsuffering . . ." (Gal 5:22).

"With all lowliness and gentleness, with longsuffering, bearing with one another in love" (Eph 4:2).

"Strengthened with all might, according to His glorious power, for all patience and longsuffering with joy" (Col 1:11).

"A quick tempered man acts foolishly" (Prov 14:17a).

"He who is slow to wrath has great understanding. But he who is impulsive exalts folly" (Prov 14:29).

"A wrathful man stirs up strife,
But he who is slow to anger allays contention" (Prov 15:18).

"The discretion of a man makes him slow to anger, And it is to his glory to overlook a transgression" (Prov 29:11).

"An angry man stirs up strife,
And a furious man abounds in transgression" (Prov 29:22).

"A fool always loses his temper,
But a wise man holds it back" (Prov 29:11 NASB).

The Lord asked Jonah, "Is it right for you to be angry?" We should remember that question the next time we are tempted to fly off the handle. We should remember that there is only the difference of a letter between anger and danger. Then we should do what Julius Caesar did: whenever he was provoked, he would repeat the whole alphabet to himself before responding.

When a friend was remonstrating with a Christian about his frightfully ungoverned temper, the culprit said, "Oh well, my spells don't last long." The friend said, "My dear man, an earthquake doesn't last long, but it does a terrible lot of damage while it's on."

CHAPTER 22

What Shall I Wear?

"WHAT? YOU mean to say that holiness has to do with the clothes that we wear? No way! It's what's inside that counts. God is only interested in what we are, not our apparel."

The argument sounds convincing, but the fact is that God is interested in both, because He knows that the outward is often a gauge of what we are inside. Listen, for instance, to the way in which He castigated the daughters of Zion:

> In that day the Lord will take away the finery: the jingling anklets, the scarves, and the crescents; the pendants, the bracelets, and the veils; the headdresses, the leg ornaments, and the headbands; the perfume boxes, the charms and the rings; the nose jewels, the festal apparel, and the mantles; the outer garments; the purses, and the mirrors, the fine linen, the turbans, and the robes. And so it shall be: instead of a sweet smell there will be a stench; instead of a sash, a rope; instead of a rich robe, a girding of sackcloth; and branding instead of beauty (Isa 3:18-24).

Why did God care? The answer is given in v. 16.

> Because the daughters of Zion are haughty, and walk with outstretched necks and wanton eyes, walking and mincing as they go, making a jingling with their feet.

Their expensive, showy apparel was an indication of their pride and vanity.

177

Tips for the Clothes Closet

So let us look at some of the principles which the Word sets forth in order for Christ to be Lord of our clothes closet.

First, our clothes should be modest and discreet. "In like manner also, that the women adorn themselves in modest apparel" (1 Tim 2:9a). "Modest" here may have different shades of meaning but it certainly includes the idea of decent. Modest clothing does not expose large areas of the human anatomy with suggestive intent. It does not make it hard for another believer to live as a Christian should.

Nor should our clothing be attention-getting or a means of self-advertisement. We are not here to attract attention to ourselves; our purpose is to glorify Christ (John 3:30; Col 1:18b). As J. Russell Howden pointed out, "The Christian's business in life is to magnify Christ, not his purse, or his tailor, or himself."

So we should avoid two extremes. On the one hand, we should not rush to imitate the world in the latest bizarre fashions. But neither should we make ourselves conspicuous by wearing clothes that are old-fashioned or dowdy. To quote Howden again, "God neither commands nor commends dowdiness or untidiness. Slovenliness in person or dress is no mark of spirituality. If our bodies are the temple of the Holy Spirit, then whatever is beautiful, lovely, and becoming properly belongs to them as such." The old rule is still applicable: "Be not the first by whom the new is tried, nor yet the last to lay the old aside."

Certainly we should have only a modest supply of

clothing. In a world of such enormous need as ours, it seems less than humane for Christians to maintain clothes closets that look like miniature department stores.

And for the same reason we should avoid buying clothing at exorbitant prices. ". . . not with braided hair or gold or pearls or costly clothing" (1 Tim 2:9b). "Do not let your beauty be that outward adorning . . . of wearing gold, or of putting on fine apparel" (1 Pet 3:3). However, that does not mean that we are always obligated to buy the cheapest product. That could be a false economy. We have to weigh price and quality. For example, if we buy the cheapest shoes, it is possible that we will pay more to a foot doctor than if we spent a little more on footwear and got a better fit and better quality.

Our clothes should be neat and clean. Dirty, shabby clothes are not a good advertisement for the Saviour. Or, as Oswald Chambers said, "Slovenliness is an insult to the Holy Spirit."

The Christian's apparel should indicate the sex of the wearer. The usual proof text for this is Deut 22:5: "A woman shall not wear anything that pertains to a man, nor shall a man put on a woman's garment, for all who do so are an abomination to the Lord your God." Primarily this verse is directed against transvestism, the adopting of the dress and often the behaviour of the opposite sex. But it would also apply to the unisex movement, the obliteration of sexual distinction by hair and clothing styles. There is no question that God hates the confusion of the sexes.

In general, our dress should be representative of the Lord whose ambassadors we are. And this may vary according to our culture and the historical period in which we live. We must remember that it is possible that our appearance may cancel out our message. Kierkegaard tells of a circus clown who was sent into a town in his costume to warn of a fire spreading from the circus tent. "The townspeople listened to his cries and roared with laughter. It was just the sort of rubbish to expect from clowns. And the town burned down because his associations cancelled out his message."

It's What's Inside

The emphasis in the Bible is on our inward character, not our outward display. Note, for instance Col 3:12-14.

> Therefore, as the elect of God, holy and beloved, put on tender mercies, kindness, humbleness of mind, meekness, longsuffering; bearing with one another, and forgiving one another, if anyone has a complaint against another; even as Christ forgave you, so you also must do. But above all these things put on love, which is the bond of perfection.

And returning to 1 Tim 2:9-10, "In like manner also, that the women adorn themselves . . . with good works."

> O worship the Lord in the beauty of holiness!
> Bow down before Him, His glory proclaim;
> With robes of obedience, and incense of lowliness,
> Kneel and adore Him; the Lord is His Name.

CHAPTER 23

To Tell the Truth

IS IT ever right to lie? There is only one answer. God cannot lie and He cannot delegate the authority to anyone else. The ninth commandment forbids bearing false witness. Christians are to put away lying and to speak truth with their neighbours (Eph 4:25). Satan is the father of lies (John 8:44) and we are not to imitate his behaviour.

Dennis J. De Haan reminds us that "dishonesty wears many masks. It makes promises without intending to keep them. It says nothing if undercharged in a checkout lane. It keeps an item acquired by mistake (a case of dishonesty giving birth to thievery). It disguises the truth to gain personal advantage. It lies to cover up wrongs."

It is true that the Bible *records* lies, but it never *approves* them. Abraham lied concerning Sarah (Gen 12:10-20; 20:2). Isaac lied about Rebekah (Gen 26:7). Ananias and Sapphira lied to God about the extent of their dedication (Acts 5:1-11).

There are other occasions when God's people didn't lie but when they didn't tell all the truth. The Hebrew midwives said that the Hebrew women delivered their babies before the midwives could get to them (Exod 1:19). The fact that God approved (v. 20) shows that they were not lying. Moses asked permission for the Israelites to go three days into the wilderness to sacrifice (Exod 5:3); he knew that if Pharaoh refused the smaller request, he would refuse the

181

greater one, that   is, permanent departure. Ehud said he had a secret message from the Lord for King Eglon; he didn't reveal that it was a message of death (Judges 3:12-30). When God told Samuel to anoint David as king, He said that if questioned by King Saul, he should simply say that he had come to sacrifice to the Lord (1 Sam 16:1-3). It was true. He did sacrifice, but that was not the whole reason for the trip. He was not obligated to tell all he knew.

Sometimes people excuse lying on the basis that the end justifies the means. Doing evil that good may come is a form of Jesuitical casuistry that is condemned in the Scriptures (Rom 3:8).

The stickiest problem of conscience in this whole area arises when human life is imperilled if we tell the truth. The classic illustration involves Christians who hid Jews during the Nazi occupation. The soldiers came to the door and asked, "Are there any Jews here?" It would be a barefaced lie to say no. Yet any other answer would mean death for the Jews and their hosts. What to do?

Some would say, "Tell the truth and leave the consequences with the Lord." This is an almost certain death sentence.

Another option is to trust God at that time to give you an answer that would be neither dishonest nor incriminating. God can do this, but has not always chosen to do so.

Others say that in a world of wickedness such as ours, it is sometimes necessary to choose the lesser of two evils. Here lying, though still wrong, would be a lesser evil than consigning innocent people to death.

The only time when this policy would be valid is when the lives of others are involved.

Others quote Acts 5:29: "We ought to obey God rather than men." God says, "You shall not murder" (Exod 20:13). He also says, "Deliver those who are drawn toward death, and hold back those stumbling to the slaughter. If you say, 'Surely we did not know this,' does not He who weighs the hearts consider it? He who keeps your soul, does He not know it?" (Prov 24:11, 12).

One final consideration. There are certain acts which are not good works in themselves but which become good works when they are a demonstration of true saving faith. Ordinarily it would have been murder for Abraham to offer Isaac as a burnt offering, but God approved it because it showed the genuineness of Abraham's faith (James 2:21). Ordinarily it would have been treason for Rahab to befriend the spies, but she was actually justified by doing it because it showed that she was a **true** believer in the Lord (James 2:25). Extract faith from these two works and they would have been evil.

As we said, the problem is a sticky one. Fortunately most of us will never have to face it. For the thousand and one problems that we will face, the solution is this: tell the truth and never lie. To quote Dennis De Haan again, "Lying undermines confidence, creates suspicion, and destroys relationships. But worst of all, it is an insult to God, who is the source of all truth."

CHAPTER 24

Moral Dilemmas

NO TREATMENT of the subject of christian holiness would be complete without a consideration of ethics, that is, the problem of what is morally good and bad, right and wrong. In every society, there are innumerable temptations and pressures to cut corners, to compromise, and to cheat. The temptation is especially strong when money is involved. That is what led Voltaire to say, "When it comes to money, all men are of the same religion." Every Christian should be committed to prove Voltaire wrong.

A businessman said his philosophy was that "business is like a folding screen; it only stands if it is crooked." Others are frank to say that they would go broke if they ran their business according to the Sermon on the Mount; in other words, they couldn't survive if they were straight.

Let us list some breaches of ethics that are common today: falsifying income tax returns; padding expense accounts; dishonest advertising; resorting to bribes, kickbacks, and payoffs; cheating on weights and measures; producing inferior merchandise; drawing cheques against an insufficient account; declaring bankruptcy to escape creditors. Other unethical practices include: plagiarism; helping oneself to the employer's office supplies or tools; failure to give sixty minutes of work for every hour of pay; witnessing for Christ in company time; withholding from the work of the Lord; disobeying traffic laws; breaking confidences; failure to keep appointments on time.

Should a christian lawyer plead not guilty for a criminal whom he knows to be guilty? Should a christian airline attendant serve liquor? How about a purchasing agent accepting gifts and gratuities from suppliers? Here is a missionary who can save days or even weeks of delay if he gives a bribe to a foreign bureaucrat; should he do it? A student has access to an exam in advance; should he take it? Is there an ethical problem in selling products that are known to produce cancer? A christian school, hard up for money, is offered £100,000 by a brewery; should the Board of Directors accept the gift? A patient insists that his christian doctor sign an insurance claim which they both know is not valid; should he sign? A supplier of building materials is on the local Board of Assessors. If contractors buy from him, they can get a reduction in their real estate taxes. They have to buy from some supplier, so why not from him?

The High Cost of Honesty and Dishonesty

Here is a Greek who owns a small restaurant. A city inspector examines the restaurant and draws up a long list of changes that must be made: a new hood for the stove, a new meat cutting block, new counters and stools, and other changes that would cost thousands. At the end, the inspector asks, "Is it worth £25 to you?" If the owner says "No," the inspector will say, "Have the work done in two weeks or close your doors."

When the Tacoma Narrows Bridge was completed,

an enterprising insurance agent was fortunate to write the policy. He was so sure that the bridge was indestructible that he pocketed the premiums. One day a strong wind set up a vibration on the structure and the bridge plummeted into the water.

There is no denying that Christians face a lot of tough decisions, but it's tougher to make the wrong one.

Here are some examples of men who had the courage to do what they knew to be right, no matter what the cost might be.

Adam Clark worked in a fabric shop. His boss instructed him to stretch the silk when he was measuring it. Adam said, "Sir, your silk will stretch, but my conscience won't." God later used Adam Clark to write a commentary on the Bible that bears his name.

In another store, a customer urged the clerk to give him an extra quantity at no extra cost. "Go ahead," the customer said, "Your boss isn't looking." The clerk replied, "*My Boss* is *always* looking!"

On a new job, Dick F..... travelled all week with his trainer. At the end of each day, his trainer would record the total time spent working at various customers' locations. Although it was often seven hours or less, he would adjust it to eight hours, and tried to get Dick to do the same for his hours. Dick protested that as a Christian, he couldn't do it, even if his job depended on it. The trainer reacted angrily, but Dick kept his job and later became a missionary to Ecuador.

When Harold G ..... was hired to deliver potato

chips to the supermarkets, he was told to carry a sharp pencil with which to puncture the bags of his competitors. The puncture allowed humid air to get in and wilt the potato chips. Harold refused and yet was not fired. Sometimes employers realise that honest men are the best kind to have.

Bob B..... worked for a men's clothing store. Once, the manager, a professing Christian, told him that they were going to have a sale of men's suits. He told Bob to take upstairs all the suits that normally sold for £150, put on new price tags marked £200, then mark them down to £175. After remonstrating with the boss, Bob resigned. God honoured him by putting him into the ministry.

God's promise is sure. "Those who honour Me, I will honour" (1 Sam 2:30). There may be a price to pay in the short run, but the Lord will always vindicate His people who act righteously.

CHAPTER 25

Lord, Break Me!

IT WAS a time when revival fires were sweeping across Ruanda, and one of the prominent features of the revival was a spirit of brokenness that was poured out on the national believers. The Rev. Kevin Baker[4] was sent out from England by his denomination to train men for the ministry.

As he taught in the seminary, his theology became increasingly liberal. He was planting doubts and denials concerning the word of God. In the class was a small group of men known as *abalokele,* that is, "born again ones". These men met for prayer every morning at 4.00. When news reached Kevin that they were praying for him, he was affronted. After all, he was a cleric of the church, and they were ignorant natives.

One day Kevin decided to call in the leader and tell him off. The national sat quietly as he was subjected to a barrage of rebuke and humiliation. At the end, all he said was, "But you really do need help." The Reverend Professor was more angry than ever.

However, as the saved ones continued to pray, God began to work in the Rev. Mr. Baker's life. He began to realise how far he had drifted from the orthodox faith. He finally became so convicted that he had to go to the Bishop and confess that his teaching, though acceptable to the church, was contrary to the truths of Scripture.

The Bishop was deeply disappointed at Kevin's

evangelical stance. He buried his face in his hands and said, "Oh Kevin, now you can never become a Bishop." Kevin said, "Praise the Lord!"

The Pressure to Break

As the Holy Spirit continued to convict him, Kevin felt pressured to go to the leader of the born again ones and apologise. How demeaning! – for him, a cleric in a prestigious denomination, to apologise to a black student. He struggled against the idea, but the pressure mounted. He was kicking against the goads. He found no peace until he decided to go. Thoroughly broken, he climbed into his car, started off, and rehearsed his little speech of apology.

As soon as he reached the door, the leader of the born again ones appeared and said, "Hallelujah!" He knew that his prayers had been answered. It was the first time Kevin had ever embraced a black man – the first time he had ever wanted to.

Now the saved ones asked Kevin to join them at the 4 a.m. prayer meeting! That was something that was completely outside his sphere as a clergyman. He sputtered a string of excuses. They listened patiently, then asked, "Would you try it for a week?" Helpless to resist any further, he agreed. Soon he experienced a spiritual exhilaration in prayer he had never known before.

When the administration heard that one of their instructors was meeting with students for prayer at 4 a.m., they considered this to be subversive to the best interests of the seminary. Their solution was to transfer the Rev. Mr. Baker to another school and to forbid any meetings on campus before 7 a.m.

The saved ones weighed the matter before the Lord, then decided they should obey God rather than man. Because they continued to pray, they were expelled from the seminary a few weeks short of graduation. But they were broken, not bitter. They took it patiently and without recriminations. But they sensed that Brother Kevin was still nursing bitter feelings toward the Bishop. So they went to him and suggested that he confess his hard attitude to the Bishop. This time Kevin did not struggle. He went quickly, cleared the record, and experienced continuous revival in his life.

Hit Him on the Heart

Of all the elements of holiness, brokenness must be one of the most important and influential. When we speak of a broken man we mean one whose will has been subdued by the will of God. He is meek and gentle in the presence of adverse circumstances and irritating people. When struck on one cheek, he turns the other. Said E. Stanley Jones:

> By turning the other cheek you disarm your enemy. He hits you on the cheek and you, by your moral audacity, hit him on the heart by turning the other cheek. His enmity is dissolved. Your enemy is gone. You got rid of your enemy by getting rid of your enmity ... The world is at the feet of the Man who had power to strike back but who had power not to strike back. That is power ... the ultimate power.

Readiness to break is a beautiful trait of character. It resists the natural impulse to retaliate, to defend self, or to complain. God is looking for broken vessels.

> Pitchers for the lamps of God!
> Hark, the cry goes forth abroad.
> Not the beauty of the make,
> But the readiness to break
> Marks the vessels of the Lord.

One day a member of his congregation came into the office of Dr. Alexander Whyte with some of the latest news. It seems that a visiting preacher had said publicly that one of Dr. Whyte's ministerial associates was not a Christian.

Dr. Whyte blazed with indignation. He was irate that such a charge should be levelled against a faithful servant of the Lord. In a few well-chosen words, he expressed his anger against the one who had been guilty of this sin.

"That isn't all," said the parishioner. "He even said that you are not a true believer either."

At that, Dr. Whyte slumped, then said, "Please leave the office so that I can be alone and examine my heart before the Lord."

Brokenness is a lesson that some of us do not learn easily. One evening I was visiting in a home with two older, respected servants of the Lord. I can't remember how the subject came up, but they started to criticise the Bible School of which I was President. I could feel a hot flush rising from my collar. I felt like a mother would feel if someone said, "My, what an ugly baby." Well, my emotions burst like a Niagara, and I let them have it, both barrels. On the way home, I rather congratulated myself that I had valiantly defended the cause of righteousness.

Some months later, I was travelling to Iowa for meetings. The Spirit of God came upon me in searing conviction. It was as if He were saying: "Here you are, MacDonald, going to tell other people how to live the christian life. Yet remember the way you spoke to those two servants of Mine, and you have never made it right." Before I could preach that weekend, I had to write a letter of apology to those men.

Brokenness Cements Relationships

Was that the end of a friendship? No, it was the beginning of an association deeper than it had ever been. They wrote a gracious letter, assuring me of their forgiveness, and assuring me of their deep interest and prayers. God's way is the best way; He knows that brokenness cements relationships whereas pride destroys them.

Well, you would think that I would have learned a lesson. But no! One morning I was preparing to participate in a funeral service when my phone rang. It was a preacher from England, visiting in the area. I happened to know that he held views on the coming of the Lord that I considered most unscriptural. Eventually the subject of prophecy came up and I vented my feelings in a rather heated manner. I'm sure the phone wires were hot. Incidentally, it was very poor preparation for a funeral. We tangled at considerable length, then concluded, each of us being more convinced than ever of his own position.

Years later I was in London. Again I had a most unwanted visit from the Lord. I was walking down a street near where this preacher lived. I can still see the telephone kiosk ahead of me. "There it is, Bill. Don't you think you should call that brother and apologise for the way you spoke to him?"

"But Lord, I still feel I was right. I was defending the truth of Your imminent return."

"That isn't the point. It's not so much a matter of truth as of attitude."

I went into the booth and dialled the number (hoping that he would not be in). But he was in. In fact, he was the one who answered. I explained why I had called. It was a blow to my pride, such a blow that my pride has never recovered. He graciously accepted my apology and arranged for me to have lunch with him the next day at a nearby restaurant. Later I was invited to speak at the assembly he attended.

But someone might be asking, "Suppose I am not broken. What can I do about it?" I would suggest four steps.

Steps to Brokenness

First pray, "Lord, break me," Recognise that you, like all other Christians, are in need of change, then pray that the Lord will produce that change in your life. But count the cost. The breaking process is painful.

Second, ransack your past for wrongs that need to be righted, for unkind words that need apology, for times when you acted in the flesh rather than in the Spirit.

Next, confess to God and then to the person or persons offended. Somehow it seems easier to confess to God than to others. But bite the bullet. Do all that needs to be done so that you can walk with an ungrieved Holy Spirit.

Finally, feel free to share your experience with others. It may not do anything for your own ego, but perhaps it will encourage them to experience the blessing that comes from brokenness.

God loves broken things and broken people. As Vance Havner wrote, "It takes broken soil to produce a crop, broken clouds to give rain, broken grain to give strength. It is the broken alabaster box that sheds forth perfume. It is Jacob limping from Jabbok who has power with God and men. It is Peter weeping bitterly who returns to greater power than ever."

Chapter 26

Substance Abuse - Just Say No!

STEVE WAS a happily-married young businessman who first had his cocaine at a friend's party. Soon he began to live for the drug's sensational but short-lived rush of power and pleasure. His £60 per day habit so consumed his home life that before long it fell apart. Like so many others, his story ended in conflict, bankruptcy and divorce. Even the friends who "turned him on" now walked out on him.

No one denies that there are pleasures connected with drugs. Even the Bible admits that the world offers pleasures but it speaks of them as the "passing pleasures of sin" (Heb 11:25). They *are* pleasures but they *don't last*. And the price men have to pay for indulging in them is too high.

What should be the attitude of believers toward the drug scene with its amphetamines, barbiturates, heroin, cocaine, PCP, opium, marijuana, LSD, peyote, glue, nitrous oxide, and prescription drugs such as codeine, Darvon and Percodan? Does the Bible have anything to say about them?

When Paul lists the works of the flesh in Galatians 5:19-21, he includes the word sorcery (v. 20) or witchcraft (NIV). In the original language of the NT, the word is *pharmakeia*[5], suggesting the use of drugs, potions, spells, or enchantments. It is a reminder that drugs are used in the magical arts, which are part of the world of demonism. Of course there is a valid use of drugs, when prescribed by a doctor, but the Bible is speaking about the use of drugs by witch doctors, spirit mediums, and others involved in spiritism.

Users are Losers

We know that mind-expanding drugs can carry the user into the realm of the transcendental and actually open his life to the entrance of demons. Some converted addicts claim that it is impossible to get hooked on drugs without at the same time becoming demon-possessed.

The goal of a demon is always to destroy (Mark 9:22; John 10:10a). There is no exception to this rule. He will seek to destroy either the drug user or some other victim. That explains many of the senseless, brutal crimes that we hear about today. It is important to recognise this link between drugs, demons, and destruction, and to avoid getting involved.

Of course, there are other reasons why a believer should stay away from harmful chemicals. They are addicting, and a Christian should not allow himself to be enslaved to any habit (Rom 6:16-23). They are expensive. In order to maintain the habit, men are often driven to theft and violence and women are sometimes driven to prostitution. Infection from needles, emaciation, damage to the immune system are only a few of the results to the body. Often the damage to the mind is irreversible. Addicts become zombies, weirdos, and suicides. Add to this the fact that the use of most drugs is illegal. Violators invite arrests, trial, heavy legal expenses, and, if convicted, imprisonment. And there is always the danger of overdose, often followed by a ride to the cemetery or crematorium.

A Christian should never use these harmful chemicals because his body is a temple of the Holy Spirit (1 Cor 6:19). Neither should he "deal" them since he would be harming others and would be giving a completely false view of what a Christian should be like. Our job is to win men to Christ, not to drug addiction.

Earlier we mentioned that there is often a link between drugs and demonism. There are other things associated with demonism which the believer should avoid: tarot cards, astrology, black magic, white magic, yoga, fortune telling, the ouija board, the crystal ball, clairvoyance, palm reading, seances, and communicating with the dead (see Deut 18:9-14).

Alcohol

When a converted drunkard was asked, "Do you believe that Jesus changed water into wine?" he replied, "Yes, I have seen Him change whisky into groceries, gambling tickets into furniture, and a broken-hearted wife into a radiant Christian. I have no difficulty believing He changed water into wine."

The most common form of drug abuse is alcohol. Like the drugs discussed in the previous section, it is an escape route from the world of reality. It provides a temporary high, a chance to forget the problems of the moment, and a relief from tension. But, like the other drugs, it is demoralising, dehumanising, and destructive.

Those who claim to be Christians must adopt a biblical view toward the subject of alcoholic beverages. God's original intention was that wine should be enjoyed by men and women, but in moderation (Ps 104:15a). He warns against overuse that results in the loss of ability to make proper decisions (Prov 31:4, 5; Hos 4:11). He permits the use of wine in areas where the water causes stomach disorders (1 Tim 5:23) and advocates its medicinal use for the dying (Prov 31:6, 7). But the danger, of course, is that people might abuse a God-given mercy by becoming alcoholics. God solemnly warns believers against over-indulgence (Rom 13:13). He clearly states that no drunkard will inherit the kingdom of God (1 Cor 6:10). Even though a man may profess to be a believer, he shows that his profession is false if he is a drunkard. When abused, "wine is a mocker, intoxicating drink arouses brawling, and whoever is led astray by it is not wise" (Prov 20:1). In cultures such as ours where drinking might stumble another person, believers should practice total abstinence, that is, stay away from intoxicating beverages completely (Rom 14:21).

Actually believers should not need to use wine as a crutch. The Apostle Paul suggests that to be filled with the Holy Spirit, rather than to be filled with wine is the way to go for a child of God (Eph 5:18).

Sickness or Sin?

Don't be deceived by the current myth that alcoholism is a sickness rather than a sin. The Bible says that it is sin, and that no drunkard will inherit the kingdom of God (1 Cor 6:10). Man is morally responsible for his behaviour and he can't escape that responsibility by renaming sin as sickness.

Some years ago *National Voice* magazine carried the following spoof on alcoholism being a sickness:

> It is the only disease that is contracted by an act of the will.
> It is the only disease that requires a licence to propagate it.
> It is the only disease that is bottled and sold.
> It is the only disease that requires outlets to spread it.
> It is the only disease that produces revenue for the government.
> It is the only disease that promotes crime.
> It is the only disease that is habit-forming.
> It is the only disease that is spread by advertising.
> It is the only disease without germ or virus cause with no human corrective medicine.
> It is the only disease that bars the patient from heaven.
> It is the only disease that is given as a Christmas present.

Drinking is an addictive habit, and a believer shouldn't allow himself to be enslaved to anything or anyone but the Lord Himself (1 Cor 9:26, 27).

It is an expensive habit, often diverting money that should be used for family or personal needs. Solomon said that anyone who loves wine (excessively) will not be rich (Prov 21:17). And the prophet Joel describes men who are so desperate for it that they will sell a girl to buy it (Joel 3:3).

The effects of alcoholism on a person's health are well known – cirrhosis of the liver, kidney trouble, heart ailments, damage to brain cells. The average life span of alcoholics in the U.S. is 51, much shorter than the national average. Alcoholism during pregnancy may prove harmful to the unborn child. Someone said, "God forgives our sins but our bodies never do."

Add to that the work hours lost, the frequent inability to hold down a job, the devastation it causes in family life, the manslaughter caused by drunk drivers, the suicides, and the murders committed when under the influence. Recent statistics show that over 80% of those locked up in jails or prisons committed their crimes while under the influence of alcohol or drugs. It all adds up to a bad scene.

Solomon gives a classic description of a drunkard in Prov 23:29-35 TEV:

> Show me someone who drinks too much,
> who has to try out fancy drinks,
> and I will show you someone miserable
> and sorry for himself, always causing trouble
> and always complaining. His eyes are bloodshot,
> and he has bruises that could have been avoided.
> Don't let wine tempt you,
> even though it is rich red,
> and it sparkles in the cup,
> and it goes down smoothly.
> The next morning you will feel as if
> you had been bitten by a poisonous snake.
> Weird sights will appear before your eyes,
> and you will not be able to think or speak clearly.

You will feel as if you were out on the ocean,
seasick, swinging high up
in the rigging of a tossing ship.
"I must have been hit," you will say.
"I must have been beaten up,
but I don't remember it.
Why can't I wake up?
I need another drink."

The Safest Policy

The only way a person can be sure that he will not become an alcoholic is by staying away from liquor completely. And this is the surest way that his behaviour will not stumble someone else. This is an important consideration for all of us. If a weak believer sees you or me taking a drink, he may conclude that if it's all right for us, then it's all right for him too. Yet he may become addicted to alcohol, ending up as a drunk. In that case, you and I are morally responsible because we set a bad example. That is why Paul said, "It is good neither to eat meat nor drink wine nor do anything by which your brother stumbles" (Rom 14:21). It is why he also said, "Therefore, if food makes my brother stumble, I will never again eat meat, lest I make my brother stumble" (1 Cor 8:13). It is worse to make men drunkards than to be one yourself – and God knows that it's bad enough to be one.

There Can Be Victory

Mel Trotter was a drunkard. To avoid the hangover that followed the cheap high, he stayed drunk all the time. One day when his baby had died, he craved a drink but was broke. So he went to the coffin, took off the baby's shoes, and pawned them for a drink. Then realising the wretchedness of what he had done, he started walking toward the lake to end it all. On the way he passed a skid row rescue mission, went in, heard the gospel, and was wonderfully saved. His life was completely changed. No longer an alcoholic, he spent the rest of his life pointing down-and-out street people to the Saviour. He was living proof that there is victory over alcoholism through the power of the Holy Spirit. He disproved the notion that an alcoholic can never be completely freed from the temptation to take a drink. Such an idea does not take account of the Spirit's power to provide deliverance.

After another drunk was converted, he asked to be baptised in order to express his death to the old way of life and his determination to walk in newness of life. Later, when the caretaker drained the baptismal tank, he found a bottle of whisky at the bottom. It was the baptised believer's way of ending that chapter in his life.

Any believer who has a problem with alcohol should follow a few simple rules:

> 1. Dump out any remaining supply of liquor which you have on hand. This will test your sincerity in desiring deliverance.
> 2. Cry to God continually for power to stay away from the bottle. Pray, "Lead me not into temptation, but deliver me from evil."
> 3. Resist every temptation to indulge – even if it's just a little drink (Prov 1:10). You can do this by calling on the Lord to help (Prov 18:10). Every

victory will help you to win over the next temptation (1 Cor 10:13).

4. Confess every failure immediately to God (1 John 1:9). It is often helpful to share failures with a spiritual, understanding Christian who will serve as a prayer partner.

5. Avoid places and persons that will bring back the old temptation (Rom 13:14).

6. If possible, be accountable to another, more mature believer who will pray with you through difficult times and be a friend to you at all times (Prov 17:17).

If you are really desperately serious about it, God will give all the needed power to overcome. But you must mean business[6].

CHAPTER 27

Gambling, the Great Rip-off

"YOU MAY have already won £100,000. Your lucky sweepstakes numbers are enclosed. Return them to us with your subscription. Join the list of winners."

With come-ons similar to this we are constantly bombarded with invitations to participate in some form of gambling. Even as we pass through the check-out aisle of the supermarket, we are given a bingo card. When we think of the soaring cost of the groceries we have just bought, the possibility of winning £1,000 or more isn't exactly repulsive.

Back home, in our Lazy-boy recliner, we read of a workman who has just won a quarter of a million in the lottery. For a relatively small bet, he wins a quarter of a million! "Wow", we think, "What couldn't I do with a quarter of a million!"

The door bell rings! A cute little girl wants you to buy a chance for a raffle at her school. Hard to refuse! A sweet child! And a worthy cause!

The Lure of the Fast Buck

Our society offers all kinds of opportunities for "getting rich quick" or making "a fast buck" or taking a chance in some game of luck. There are the horse races and dog races. There is the big-time gambling at the casinos with their roulette wheels and slot machines (one-armed bandits). There are national lotteries, state lotteries and the Irish Sweepstakes. There are the ubiquitous bingo games, sponsored more often than not by churches. You can bet on football games, baseball games, boxing matches. You can play the numbers game, or card games, such as blackjack and five-card stud. Or, if you want something more sophisticated, you can speculate in the stock market. This is not to say that all stock market transactions are gambling; they are not. They might be very conservative investments. It depends on the motive of the buyer and the nature of the stock.

The lure of gambling is that the possible returns are vastly out of proportion to the amount of the bet. In 1975 a Brazilian named Miron de Souza bet the equivalent of thirty pence in a football pool and won $2,451,549. It was the world's biggest gambling win up to that time.

The following year a twenty-six year old New Jersey man won a state lottery entitling him to $1,776 a week for the rest of his life. If he lives to be 76, he will have received a total of $4.6 million.

Since then the winnings in lotteries have sky-rocketed. And the higher they go, the more people are lured to become involved.

Insights from the Word

What does the Bible have to say about all this? Is gambling in any form a legitimate activity for anyone who bears the name of Christian?

While the Bible does not explicitly say, "You shall not gamble," the tenth commandment does say, "You shall not covet" (Exod 20:17). Gambling is a form of covetousness. It expresses an inordinate desire for wealth, and a dissatisfaction with what God's providence has given me. It means that I want to enrich myself at the expense of others, if possible. And it means that I look to chance and fortune rather than to my heavenly Father.

Therefore, all the Bible prohibitions against covetousness apply to gambling. In Luke 12:15, for instance, we read, "Beware, and be on your guard against every form of greed; for not even when one has an abundance does his life consist of his possessions" (NASB). The believer's way of life should be free from the love of money; he should be content with what he has (Heb 13:5). Covetousness is idolatry (Col 3:5); as mentioned above, it dethrones God from the soul, and puts the desire for more in His place. Covetousness is ranked with immorality, drunkenness and swindling as a sin for which a person can be excommunicated from the local assembly (1 Cor 5:11). In fact, it is of such evil magnitude that it will exclude a person from the kingdom of God forever (1 Cor 6:10).

The Bible also says, "Wealth gained by dishonesty will be diminished: but he who gathers by labour will increase" (Prov 13:11). Whereas honourable work is creative and productive, gambling is not. The "take" in gambling has a way of "taking off."

The Bible says, "A man with an evil eye hastens after riches, and does not consider that poverty will come upon him" (Prov 28:22). The motive in gambling is greed. Since greed is impure and sinful, it invites the curse of God. In this case, the curse of God is poverty.

The Bible says, "As a partridge that broods but does not hatch, so is he who gets riches but not by right: it will leave him in the midst of his days, and at his end he will be a fool" (Jer 17:11). The money won by gambling does not provide lasting satisfaction; it is more apt to bring a torrent of trouble.

After reminding Timothy that the believer should be content with food and raiment, Paul warned that those who desire to be rich "fall into temptation and a snare, and into many foolish and harmful lusts which drown men in destruction and perdition" (1 Tim 6:9).

Gambling will always have an evil connotation for believers when they remember how Roman soldiers gambled for the Saviour's seamless robe at the scene of His crucifixion (John 19:23, 24).

A Losing Business

When people hit the jackpot, their "good luck" is well publicised. But the losses from gambling are strangely soft-pedalled. We seldom hear about the Italian businessman who lost $1,920,000 at a roulette table in Monte Carlo in 1974. Or the Arab prince who lost more than $1 million in a single session at Las Vegas that same year. We seldom hear of the billions that are lost by average citizens every year as they bet their hard-earned wages, with the odds stacked against them. Mathematically their chances of winning are pathetically small. The world's largest slot machine, for instance, could conceivably pay off £1 million for a £10 investment, but the chances of its doing so are one in 25,000,000,000.

Gambling can easily become addictive. It is not uncommon for people to become transfixed, squandering their money hour after hour. They act as if they were in a trance. They probably reason that the longer they stay at it, the greater their chances of striking it rich or at least making up their losses. Occasionally they win a pittance – just enough to spur them on to further losses. No believer should allow himself to be brought under the power of gambling. Paul warned the Corinthians against anything that might be enslaving, even things that are legitimate in themselves - which gambling is not (1 Cor 6:12b).

No one can estimate the poverty and grief that chronic gamblers bring to themselves and to their families. The house falls into disrepair, the food supply dwindles, mountainous debts accumulate, while the income is wasted in a ceaseless, futile attempt to change overnight from poverty to wealth.

Consider also the crimes that have been committed in an effort to recoup losses. Theft, embezzlement, blackmail – a pandora's box of wrongs are resorted to in a frantic attempt to gain financial respectability.

Add to this the evil associations frequently linked to gambling. The involvement of the Syndicate or Mafia in organised gambling is well known. Can the Christian justify his participation in that which has the smell of hell?

Sometimes, of course, the temptation comes in a

very religious guise. Just think how much you could do with the money in the work of the Lord! It is the old sophistry of doing evil that good may come. A pious matron once came bustling up to a preacher with what she thought was the greatest idea since sliced bread. She asked him to pray that the ticket she had bought in the national lottery would be a winner. If he prayed and if she won, she promised that she would divide half the amount with the church. He replied, "I will pray that you will get a new conception of religion in general and of Christianity in particular." The work of God doesn't need money made from gambling, and God couldn't bless it anyway, because it is unsanctified money.

Those who are tempted to gamble should take to heart Paul's words, "Godliness with contentment is great gain" (1 Tim 6:6). If you are godly and content, you have something that money can't buy. If you are godly, you won't gamble, and if you are content you will have neither the need nor the desire.

Finally, those who are tempted to gamble should consider the words of Samuel Johnson, "The lust for gold, unfeeling and remorseless, is the last corruption of degenerate man".[7]

CHAPTER 28

Birth Control, Pro and Con

DOES A chapter on birth control really belong in a book on Christian holiness? Because many believers feel that it involves serious moral and ethical principles, they have urged that it be included.

The sides are drawn. There are those who feel strongly that birth control is contrary to God's will for His people. Others are equally convinced that it is not a matter of black and white but rather a subject on which each believer must be fully persuaded in his own mind (Rom 14:5).

The Case Against the Practice

Perhaps the best approach is to marshal the arguments that are most commonly used by opponents and proponents. First of all, then, the case against birth control.

1. In Gen 1:28 God said, "Be fruitful and multiply; fill the earth and subdue it." This has never been revoked.

> *Answer* (from the other side): The command was given at the dawn of creation, and then after the flood. The need for population is no longer present.

2. Large families are a sign of the Lord's blessing.

> Behold, children are a heritage from the Lord, the fruit of the womb is His reward. Like arrows in the hand of a warrior, so are the children of one's

> youth. Happy is the man who has his quiver full of
> them; they shall not be ashamed, but shall speak
> with their enemies in the gate (Ps 127:3-5).

> Your wife shall be like a fruitful vine in the very
> heart of your house, your children like olive plants
> all around your table. Behold, thus shall the man
> be blessed who fears the Lord (Ps 128: 3,4).

3. Children in a large family generally develop well-
rounded personalities, get the rough edges knocked
off, learn to think of others, and are not so apt to be
spoiled.

4. Onan is a scriptural example of one who practised birth control and was condemned by God (Gen
38:1-11).

> *Answer:* Not really, Onan's sin was his selfish
> unwillingness to marry his brother's widow, as
> levirate custom required at that time.

5. Paul wrote to the Corinthians:
Do not deprive one another except with consent for a
time, that you may give yourselves to fasting and
prayer; and come together again so that Satan does
not tempt you because of your lack of self-control (1
Cor 7:5).

> *Answer:* The subject here is the marriage act,
> which may or may not involve the use of
> contraceptives.

6. It is through childbearing that a woman finds her
principal fulfilment in life. It is in this way she is

saved as far as her position in the church is concerned (1 Tim 2:15). The role of raising up a godly seed is a tremendously important one. God's desire is that women should bear children and raise them for His glory (1 Tim 3:15; 5:14; Titus 2:4).

> *Answer:* But what about women who never have a chance to be married and to raise children?

7. It is God who opens and closes the womb (Gen 20:18; 29:31; 1 Sam 1:6), and He has not delegated this authority to man. You will search the Scripture in vain for any suggestion of birth control. Not one argument in favour of birth control is based on Scripture.

The Pro's of Birth Control

Now we turn to the arguments in favour of birth control.

1. This is an area in which the Bible does not clearly legislate. God gives a married couple freedom to seek His specific will for their lives.

2. The population explosion demands that there be some measure of control. Vast numbers of people die daily of starvation, and millions are malnourished. If the present trend is not checked, there will be worldwide catastrophe.

> *Answer:* The problem is not with the food supply but with the greed that prevents its distribution and with false religions that forbid eating meats and other forms of nutrition.

3. The number of children in a family should be limited by the financial status of the parents. It is not Christ-honouring to bring more children into the world than one can properly care for.

> *Answer:* God is as able to provide for a large family as for a small one. See Matt 6:33; Phil 4:19.

4. It may be desirable to have a large family in an agricultural society where the children can help with the work on the farm. But it is different for city dwellers with small homes and cramped apartments.

5. Procreation is not the sole purpose of marriage. God wants His people to enjoy companionship and pleasure, and to achieve unity.

6. Certainly where the mother's health is threatened, birth control is in order. If there, why not elsewhere?

7. Some feel it is undesirable to bring children into this world of sin, violence, and misery.

> *Answer:* God's mercy endures to children's children (Ps 103:17).

8. The debate is academic. It appears that almost everyone practises birth control one way or another since we no longer see families of 17, 18 and 19.

> *Answer:* The fact that "everyone's doing it" does not make it right.

9. One final consideration. Although the Bible does not explicitly teach birth control, it does teach *self-control* as one of the fruits of the Spirit (Gal 5:23b).

These then are some of the arguments pro and con. What is the final answer? The answer is for a married couple to weigh these arguments in the presence of the Lord, then pray that He will show them clearly which way He wants them to go.

It must be admitted that there are good, spiritual Christians on both sides of this issue. Whenever this is true, it is best not to be too dogmatic, or to force our convictions on others. We should admit that there are arguments on both sides and give our opponents credit for doing what they think is right in the sight of the Lord.

Chapter 29

Politics

SHOULD A Christian become engaged in politics?

Those who say yes invariably quote the familiar aphorism, "All that is necessary for evil to triumph is for good men to do nothing." If that does not clinch the case, they cite Joseph, Moses, and Daniel as examples of believers who were involved in the political system.

Although the aphorism sounds convincing, we should remember that it is a statement of human wisdom, not divine revelation. We should not give it the authority of Scripture. As for Joseph and Daniel, they never ran for office but served as government employees. Moses was more of a gadfly to the government than a part of it.

The Biblical Answer

If we go to the Word for an answer, what do we find?

The Lord Jesus did not engage in politics. If anything, He found Himself in an adverse relationship to the system.

The disciples did not engage in politics. Did they miss God's best by concentrating on the gospel?

The Apostle Paul did not engage in politics. Faithfulness to his calling and to his message pitted him against the pharisaic society.

Jesus taught that His kingdom is not of this world (John. 18:36). He said to His unbelieving brothers,

"The world cannot hate you, but it hates Me because I testify of it that its works are evil" (John 7:7).

The apostle John reminds us that "the whole world lies under the sway of the evil one" (1 John 5:19). Politics is part of the world system.

We have to separate ourselves from the world in order to influence it (2 Cor 6:17). Archimedes said he could move the world if he could get a fulcrum outside it. We must position ourselves outside the world system if we are going to move it for God.

Paul insisted that "no one engaged in warfare entangles himself with the affairs of this life" (2 Tim 2:4). All believers are (or should be) on active duty. They should not allow themselves to be distracted.

Politics is corrupt. It is a system of compromise. Decisions are commonly made on the basis of what is expedient rather than what is right. It adheres to human rather than divine principles. The late Senator Vandenberg of Michigan said, "Politics by its very nature is corrupt. The church should not forget its true function by trying to participate in an area of human affairs where it must be a poor competitor ... It will lose its purity of purpose by participating."

The Banana Project

God's solution to the world's problems is not political but spiritual. New birth rather than newly elected officials is His answer. Politics is nothing more than a band-aid on a cancer. Our marching orders are, "Let the dead bury their own dead, but you go and preach the kingdom of God" (Luke 9:60). The story of the banana peel puts things in proper perspective.

Once a man had a very important job in the publishing business and he was responsible for the publication and distribution of thousands of pieces of literature. On a particular day, he was on his way to work and as he passed a certain downtown corner he came across a banana peel on the sidewalk. Knowing of course that this was a potential danger, he took time to kick it into the gutter where no one would slip on it. But he began to think that more banana peel might be lying on the sidewalks of this large city. Suppose there was one that no one kicked in the gutter and someone stepped on it. Perhaps he should take the time to look through the streets of the city for a lurking banana peel. Otherwise someone might break some bones. Many might be saved a trip to the hospital. But wait a minute – he had his own responsibility. He was an important figure in the publishing business. It was his responsibility to keep the presses rolling and send messages to the ends of the earth. Reluctantly he abandoned the banana project for the more essential one. Let the street sweepers take care of the banana peel. That was their job.

Now let's make the application. A Christian has the greatest responsibility in the world, that is, to publish the glad tidings of the Lord Jesus Christ. This is a big business for the Christian. If he doesn't do it, it will never be done. That's why Jesus said, "Seek first the kingdom of God and His righteousness." Many people are being involved in politics ... but God has charged us with the blessed task of giving out the gospel to dying men and women. Other projects may be worthy, but if we fail in this, no one will take our place.

God's purpose in this age is not to make the world a better place to live in, but to call out of the nations a people for His name (Acts 15:14). We should be working with Him in the accomplishment of this goal. Jowett said it well: "We are partners with God in the world's redemption. This is our errand ... to anoint men in the Name of the Lord to royalty of life, to sovereignty over self, to service for the realm." He goes on to mourn the tragedy of Christians who fail to appreciate their high calling, who hug the subordinate, who creep instead of fly, who are slaves instead of kings.

The Christian's primary citizenship is heavenly (Phil 3:20). He is a pilgrim and stranger in this world (1 Pet 2:11). While he has a responsibility to obey the government and a right to use its judicial processes, he is not obligated to become a part of the system.

If I participate in politics, I am casting a vote of confidence in its ability to solve the world's problems. I have no reason for such confidence after centuries of political failure.

The general tenor of the NT is that conditions are not going to get better (1 Tim 4:1-3; 2 Tim 3:1-5). This makes the Christian's responsibility to the Great Commission all the more urgent.

Does all this mean that believers adopt a do-nothing approach? No! The point is that we can do more through prayer than we ever could through the ballot. We hold the balance of power through prayer. We can affect the destiny of nations through prayer. "The weapons of our warfare are not carnal but mighty in God for pulling down strongholds" (2 Cor 10:4).

The time hasn't come for Christians to rule (1 Cor 4:8). Lifetime is training time for reigning time. Said William Kelly:

> Never have Christians meddled with governing the world, save to His dishonour and their own shame. They are now called to suffer with Christ, by-and-by they shall reign with Him. Even He has not yet taken His great power for reigning. He sits upon His Father's throne, as the earth-rejected Christ, waiting for the word from His Father to execute judgment and sit on His own throne (Rev 3:21).

Even as I am writing this, I received a news clipping which supports Kelly's position. It says:

> Van Dyke, a born-again Christian, was a controversial figure. His political career was marked with scandal. He was nearly expelled by the Legislature in 1984 for using fraudulent campaign literature. The Public Disclosure Commission fined him $500 and the Legislature demanded an apology.

Kelly's statement is worth pondering: "Never have Christians meddled with governing the world, save to His dishonour and their own shame."

CHAPTER 30

Self-occupation, the Traitor Within

IN THE pursuit of holiness there are few things more debilitating than occupation with self. Those who look inside for victory are looking in the wrong place; they invite disappointment, discouragement, and defeat.

The world emphasises man and his potential. In its pathetic desire for recognition, popularity, and acceptance, the me-too church follows suit. It preaches secular humanism, faintly disguised in evangelical language. Religious publishers rush into print with a rash of new books on self-esteem. In a single visit to a christian bookstore, I came across the following titles:

> *Love Yourself*
> *The art of Learning to Love Yourself*
> *Self-Love, the Dynamic Force of Success*
> *I'm OK, You're OK*
> *Who Says I'm OK?*
> *A True View of You*
> *Make Friends with Your Shadow*
> *The Art of Understanding Yourself*
> *Understanding Your Past, the Key to Your Future*
> *My Beautiful Feeling*
> *You Can Feel Good About Yourself*
> *30 Days to a Less Stressful You*
> *You're Someone Special*

> *Do I Have to Be Me? (Living with Yourself and Liking It)*

Only one thin voice of protest appeared on the shelves. It was titled:

> *Leave Yourself Alone*

A great deal of modern counselling turns the searchlight in on self. The patient is told to examine his upbringing (with emphasis on his parents' colossal failures), his thoughts, motives, fears, hang-ups, and inhibitions (especially in the area of sex). As he talks out his problems in non-directive counselling, the answers appear – or so it is alleged.

The World An Insane Asylum

The Norwegian dramatist Ibsen tells the story of Peter Gynt going to a mental hospital and surprisedly finding that no one in the place seemed crazy. They all talked so sensibly and discussed their plans with such precision and concern that he felt sure they must be sane. He spoke to the doctor about it. "They're mad," said the doctor. "They talk very sensibly, I admit, but it is all about themselves. They are, in fact, most intelligently obsessed with self. It's self – morning, noon and night. We can't get away from self here. We lug it along with us, even through our dreams. O yes, young sir, we talk sensibly, but we're mad right enough."

The world is much like the hospital visited by

Peter Gynt. It seems sane enough until we realize it is possessed with itself. All it talks about are its feelings, its politics, its wars, its budgets, its money. The largest part of existence, God, is unmentioned.[8]

It is characteristic of people who suffer from mental, nervous or emotional disorders that self is the centre and circumference of their lives. Counselling techniques that encourage them to engage in introspection serve only to intensify their misery. You've heard the proverb: "Neurotics are people who build castles in the air; psychotics are those who move into them; and psychiatrists are the ones who collect the rent."

The Miserable Man of Psalm 77

There are two classic Bible passages that deal with selfism and its remedy. The first is Ps 77, which Bullinger has outlined as follows:

> Occupation with self, vv. 1-6
> Its sure result, Misery, vv. 7-9
> Occupation with God, vv. 10-12
> Its sure result, Happiness, vv. 13-20

Someone else has captioned these four sections:

> Sighing
> Sinking
> Singing
> Soaring

In the first half of the Psalm, Asaph is suffering from "I trouble," or an overdose of "vitamin I." The first personal pronouns (I, me, my) occur twenty-two times, whereas God is referred to only thirteen times. The psalmist becomes so obsessed with self that He even questions the goodness, grace, and mercy of the Most High.

In the second half, Asaph gets his eyes on the Lord. He mentions God (nouns and pronouns) twenty-four times, and makes only three personal references.

The Wretched Man of Romans 7

The second Bible passage is Rom 7:9-25. After over forty uses of the personal pronouns, Paul groans, "O wretched man that I am!" He finds no victory in self. Rather he confidently affirms, "I know that in me (that is, in my flesh) nothing good dwells". But at the end of the chapter, he turns away from self and finds victory in the Lord Jesus Christ.

Looking within for victory is like casting your anchor inside the boat; it guarantees spiritual drift.

Israel's king realized that he needed someone bigger than himself; he said, "From the end of the earth I will cry to You, when my heart is overwhelmed; lead me to the rock that is higher than I" (Ps 61:2), The Rock, of course, is God.

Self-occupation makes a person forget the blessings of the Lord and makes him ungrateful for them. It causes paralysis as far as effective service is concerned by reducing powers of concentration and the quality of work. It makes one callously insensitive to the needs of others.

The Self-centred Slave

The self-centred person is a slave to his own emotions and feelings. He is unattractive company as far as others are concerned. He wants to pour out his litany of woe to an endless number of counsellors and friends, desiring an audience but spurning advice. He has a will of iron that resists change and refuses to accept God's will. He is like the people whom the Lord describes in Ezek 33:31, 32:

> So they come to you as people do, they
> sit before you as My people, and they
> hear your words, but they do not do
> them; for with their mouth they show
> much love, but their hearts pursue their
> own gain.
>
> Indeed you are to them as a very lovely
> song of one who has a pleasant voice
> and can play well on an instrument:
> for they hear your words, but they do
> not do them.

So much for the pathology of me-ism. How can a person beat it?

Five Steps to Deliverance

First, he can turn from self-occupation to occupation with Christ (2 Cor 3:18). It is by gazing on Him that we become transformed into His likeness. A thousand good versions of self are not worth one version of Christ. Or, put another way, a sanctified self is a poor substitute for a glorified Christ. He can pray continually:

O to be saved from myself, dear Lord.
O to be lost in Thee.
O that it may be no more I
But Christ who lives in me.

                              A.B. Simpson

He should remember the true formula: Occupation with self brings distress. Occupation with others brings discouragement. Occupation with Christ brings delight.

Paul Van Gorder writes:

> The kind of attitude we need is seen in the following story. After a performance of Beethoven's Ninth Symphony, the audience gave conductor Arturo Toscanini and the musicians a prolonged ovation. Toscanini, filled with emotion, turned to his musicians and whispered, "I am nothing, you are nothing." Then, in almost adoring tones, Toscanini said, "But Beethoven is everything."

But someone may object that a certain amount of self-examination is necessary, and is even called for in the Bible. Granted. But then he should follow McCheyne's rule: "For every look you take at yourself, take ten looks at Christ." As an old hymn says, "How sweet away from self to flee, and shelter in the Saviour."

A second thing a person can do is take a biblically balanced view of himself. On the one hand he realises that he is saved by the grace of God, forgiven, justified and made fit for heaven. He stands before God in all the acceptability of God's beloved Son. He is complete in Christ, a co-heir of God and a joint-heir with Jesus Christ. He is a unique creation of

God and has a distinct role to fulfil in life. He is of great value to God and this makes him desire to be all that he can be for Jesus.

On the other hand he acknowledges that in and of himself he is nothing (2 Cor 12:11; Gal 6:3) and that in his flesh dwells no good thing. He doesn't look for good in himself, and is never disappointed when he doesn't find it there.

A third suggestion. The self-centred person should lose himself in a life of service for others. Those who find fulfilment are those who are so absorbed in helping others that they have no time to be thinking about themselves. Fulfilment comes from self-denial rather than self-occupation. This is what Jesus meant when He said, "He who loves his life will lose it, and he who hates his life in this world will keep it for eternal life" (John 12:25). When psychiatrist Karl Menninger was asked what he would do if he knew he was going to have a nervous breakdown, he said, "I'd go and find someone in worse condition than myself and try to help him."

He doesn't waste time wishing that he was someone else. In spite of physical appearance, handicaps, or limited abilities, he accepts himself as God has accepted him and says, "By the grace of God I am what I am" (1 Cor 15:10a). If there are things in life that cannot be changed, he accepts them and thus finds peace. In the areas of life that are fixed by divine sovereignty, complaining is sin and wishing it was different is futile.

Finally he should avoid things that make him introspective – whether "how-to" books on self esteem, seminars on possibility thinking, or counselling that is self-directed instead of God-directed. What we want is to forget self and concentrate on the Lord, Who is worthy.

CHAPTER 31

Take Time to be Holy

IT IS remarkable how William D. Longstaff was able to combine the essentials for a holy life in four verses of a hymn. Too often we sing the hymn without appreciating how very perceptive and comprehensive it is. In closing our study of christian holiness, let us examine it line by line and see how it embraces most of the major subjects we have been considering in the preceding chapters.

Take time to be holy. A holy life must be cultivated. It is not the product of a moment. In an age of instant-everything, we are tempted to think that a single crisis experience will produce a giant step forward in sanctification. But it doesn't work that way. It is a moment-by-moment experience of the indwelling Christ. Said Vance Havner, "It takes time to be holy and we don't have time! Happy is that soul that rekindles the fire of a simpler faith, refuses to sell out to the promoters of Progress, and still seeks the old paths to find rest within."

Speak oft with thy Lord. Without prayer there is no holiness. Prayer changes not only things but us as well. It should not be intermittent but frequent. It should not be casual but blood-earnest. It should not be forced but forceful.

Abide in Him always. Abiding speaks of continuance, and especially continuance in the life of obedience to the Word. This produces an ever-deepening knowledge of the Saviour and an ever-increasing likeness to Him. Jesus said, "If you keep My commandments, you will abide in My love, just as I have kept my Father's commandments and abide in His love" (John 15:10).

And feed on His Word. We should read, study, memorise, meditate on, and obey the Bible. Jeremiah fed on the Word and it became the joy and rejoicing of his heart. The psalmist fed on it and found that it kept him from sinning. We feed on it and find that it is "profitable for doctrine, for reproof, for correction, for instruction in righteousness."

Make friends of God's children. Fellowship with the saints has a tremendously sanctifying influence on our lives. Just as evil companions corrupt good habits, so good fellowship strengthens godly behaviour patterns.

Help those who are weak. We can extend this to describe a life of service for the Lord and for one's fellows. We have seen that idleness is a snare. Temptations are strongest when we are not actively engaged in the King's business.

Forgetting in nothing His blessing to seek. One of the tests of christian conduct is, "Can I bow my head and ask God to bless it?" Whatever we do, we should do for His glory and with a single, pure desire to please Him. He can only bless what is consistent with His own holiness.

Take time to be holy, the world rushes on. Wordsworth was right:

> The world is too much with us; late and soon,
> Getting and spending we lay waste our powers:

Spend much time in secret with Jesus alone. W. Graham Scroggie urged, "Isolate yourself for the purpose of blessing." The holiest people are those who meditate much on the Word. Unless our roots are deep in God, our lives will be superficial.

By looking to Jesus like Him thou shalt be. Almost two thousand years ago, the apostle Paul wrote, "... we all with unveiled face, beholding as in a mirror the glory of the Lord, are being transformed into the same image from glory to glory, just as by the Spirit of the Lord" (2 Cor. 3:18). In other words, we are changed into His likeness by beholding Him.

Thy friends, in thy conduct, His likeness shall see. When Moses came down from Sinai, his face glowed with borrowed radiance. When the rulers of Israel saw the boldness of Peter and John, they realized that these homespun and untrained men had been with Jesus. As we live in close communion with the Saviour, those around us will see the reflection of His moral likeness in us.

Take time to be holy, let Him be thy guide. This means nothing less than turning the controls of our life over to the Lord. It means exchanging our will for His. It means trusting His sight rather than our own.

And run not before Him whatever betide. When guidance does not come immediately, the natural reaction is to act impulsively. Like a horse champing at the bit, we take matters in our own hands. Impatient of delay, we charge ahead. The inevitable result is that we lie down in sorrow (Isa 50:11).

In joy or in sorrow still follow the Lord. Piety

should be independent of circumstances and free from ups and downs. That is why John Wesley prayed, "Lord, cure me of my intermittent piety and make me thoroughly Christian."

And, looking to Jesus, still trust in His Word. The poet keeps coming back to the Word, knowing that the Bible is the instrument God uses in cleansing and sanctifying His people. In this he parallels the sentiments of the author of Ps 119.

Take time to be holy, be calm in thy soul. The holy life is the life of peace; poise and tranquillity. Faith delivers us from panic and fretfulness. If we are truly trusting, we won't be worrying.

Each thought and each temper beneath His control. Thus David prayed, "Search me, O God, and know my heart; try me and know my anxieties; and see if there is any wicked way in me, and lead me in the way everlasting" (Ps 139: 23, 24).

> Search all my thoughts, the secret springs,
>   The motives that control;
> The chambers where polluted things
>   Hold empire o'er my soul.
>
> F. Bottome

Thus led by His Spirit to fountains of love,

Thou soon shall be fitted for service above. Which is another way of saying that when we take time to be holy, we will enjoy constant blessings in this life and be prepared for endless service in the mansions of glory. It is what Paul said to Timothy: Godliness has "promise of the life that now is and of that which is to come" (1 Tim 4:8).

The Last Word

BE HOLY may be the forgotten command but it shouldn't be. It ranks high among the commandments of the Lord. It was not given as a suggestion or even as an option but as an imperative. Like all His commands, it was given for our good and not His.

There is no higher aim than to be like the Lord Jesus. Nothing tells for God in an age of fact like a holy life. It makes Christianity credible. It glorifies God and benefits the believer. On the other hand, there is nothing that brings shame, dishonour, and reproach on the name of the Lord like a sinning saint.

Nothing should motivate us to holiness as much as the love of Christ, the price He paid for our salvation, the grace He has showered on us. Add to this the fact that sin breaks fellowship with God, stumbles others, and seals the lips.

Holiness is a process, not an achievement. We will never be absolutely holy until we see the Saviour's face, but we should be becoming increasingly like Him until then.

In the ding-dong battle against the world, the flesh, and the devil, we need to wear the armour of the christian soldier. In short that armour is a righteous christian character. As long as we wear that, our foes have little to shoot at.

Only God can make us holy, but He does not do it without our cooperation. He has given us certain principles to guide us. As we obey them, the Spirit transforms us from one degree of glory to another. Some of the prerequisites are confession, restitution, surrender, Bible study, prayer, fellowship with other Christians, service for the Lord, and a disciplined body and mind.

Holiness has to do with our sex life, our speech, our temper, and our clothing. In fact, what area of life does it *not* have to do with?

Every Christian should be jolted when he reads that without holiness, no one will ever see the Lord (Heb 12:14). This certainly includes the positional sanctification which a person receives when He trusts the Saviour. But it also embraces the practical holiness which is the invariable result of genuine conversion.

Endnotes

Chapter 13

[1]From the author's *Enjoying the Psalms* (Kansas City, KS: Walterick Publishers, 1977), Vol. 1, pp. 238-40. Used by permission.

Chapter 18

[2]Quoted by J. Oswald Sanders in *The Best That I Can Be* (Singapore: OMF Books, 1965), pp. 110, 111.

[3]Quoted in *1200 More Notes, Quotes and Anecdotes* by A. Naismith, p.93.

Chapter 25

[4]The story is true; the name Kevin Baker is fictitious.

Chapter 26

[5]Our word *pharmacy* is merely an Anglicised form of this word.

[6]This chapter is from the author's *Doing Time With Jesus,* an Emmaus Correspondence course, by the author, Emmaus Bible College, 1985.

Chapter 27

[7]This chapter is from *Gambling and Drinking,* by William MacDonald, Arthur Wilder, and Donald Norbie (Published by Everyday Publications, Scarborough, Ontario, Canada, 1980).

Chapter 30

[8]Eugene H. Peterson, *Travelling Light* (Downer's Grove, IL: InterVarsity Press), pp. 69-71.